Addie L. Ballou

Driftwood

Addie L. Ballou

Driftwood

ISBN/EAN: 9783743303690

Manufactured in Europe, USA, Canada, Australia, Japa

Cover: Foto ©Thomas Meinert / pixelio.de

Manufactured and distributed by brebook publishing software (www.brebook.com)

Addie L. Ballou

Driftwood

To My Children, and—

To those who suffer long and wait,
   Who climb, and fall, and rise again,
Who bow before imperious fate,
   But bravely court her happier vein;

To those whose lifted hands implore
   Heaven's guidance o'er the rugged way;
Who shrink when tempests round them roar,
   But steadfast wait the rising day;

To humble hearts along life's shore
   Who garner what the sea upheaves,
I dedicate in broken lore,
   With loving trust, these " Driftwood " leaves.

                        THE AUTHOR.

H

	PAGE
Hail to the Hero!	45
Her Letter	86
Home Memories	18

I

In Memoriam	65-178
Insomnia	101

K

Knights of Pythias	107

L

L'Envoi	54
Lines	17
Lines in a Portfolio	150
Long Ago	209
Lou's Christmas Gift	47
Love Never Sleeps	227

M

Major Pauline Cushman	27
Memorial Poem No. 1	185
" " " 2	189
" " " 3	194
My Ambition	146
My Dream of St. Valentine	155
My Heart Would Have Me Love You	236

N

Not Alone with the Night	158
Number Forty-four	22

O

Oh, Where are the Little Boys?	80
Open the Blind	83
Our Baby	78
Our Molly	15

P

Perdita	75
Put off at Honolulu	10

R

	PAGE
Reception to Paul Vandervoort, Grand Commander, G. A. R.	211
Reply to a Letter Requiring Extra Postage	41

S

Saint Margaret	216
Since Mother Died	92
Sleep On	71
Song of Victory	63
Song Story for the Little Ones	160
Spirit of Love	13

T

Take Courage	105
Terra Australis	56
The Battle of Ships on Mobile Bay	167
The Charge upon the Hill	204
The Coming Man	49
The " Little Matron's " Greeting	30
The Maniac's Last Hour	99
The Old and the New	221
The Tale of a Toad	43
The World must have its Crucified	137
Thorns Intertwine the Crown of Bay	175
To Arms!	62
To " Beeswax "	134
To Winnebago Lake	231
Two Sides	233

V

Violets	9

W

Wedding Anniversary	127
Welcome to Grant	114
Where do the Sea-gulls Go?	151
Which do You Choose to Wear?	59
Wormwood	154

Y

Your Praise	79

DRIFTWOOD.

DRIFTWOOD.

VIOLETS.

(FOR EVANGELINE.)

Through the long days of the chill wintry weather,
   Coyly their purple lips whisper and wait.
Under their leaflets green, huddled together,
   Violets bloom, though the spring cometh late.

Out from the south-land with sun-lighted tresses,
   Cometh the trail of the fairy of spring;
Over their beds, with her love-warm caresses,
   Perfumes of violet rise to her wing.

Out of the chill of the heart's bleak December,
   Like the bloom of the violet, tender and fair;
Though severed by oceans, love still will remember,
   And bless with devotion the friendship we share.

Nov. 23, 1894.

PUT OFF AT HONOLULU.

I'VE heard it said in Frisco rings—
   It may be false (it may be true, though)—
That king Claus Spreckles rules the sea,
   From Frisco down to Honolulu.

That steamers of the "O and O"
   (Except one buy to Sydney through, tho')
Will sell no tickets on their line
   To passengers for Honolulu.

With "All aboard!" and "All ashore!"
   How shrilly then the whistle blew, too;
The Captain said we'd next sight land,
   And stop an hour at Honolulu.

And so we sailed away, away!
   In spite of all precautions due, though,
And much against his will; 'twas said
   We'd land one soul at Honolulu.

For when the purser's round was made
    For tickets (how the Captain flew, though),
For one no ticket had, nor cash,
    To pay as far as Honolulu.

We thought the man was but a crank.
    Not so thought all the merry crew, though.
"I'll put you off," the Captain said,
    "When we arrive at Honolulu."

The fellow walked about the decks
    As bold as any Robin Crusoe,
Nor seemed to break his heart at all
    At being left at Honolulu.

They locked him up a while below;
    Of course they fed the fellow, too, though;
'Twould hardly do to starve the man
    Before we came to Honolulu.

And when we reached that tropic isle,
    We did as all good people do, do—
We went ashore to do the town,
    And do the king, at Honolulu.

Then down the gang-plank sped the man,
With "Thank ye, Captain, and adieu, too;
I'll go ashore, of course.   Ye see,
I live right here at Honolulu."

On board steamer Zealandia, of the " O and O,"
mid-ocean, June 23d, 1885.

SPIRIT OF LOVE.

I woke, and, lo!
From the deep chambers of my soft repose,
   Silent and slow,
Clothed in a mist of light, a vision rose.

   My steadfast eyes
Gazed on its splendor with new-born delight;
   As summer skies
Bedew the rose, so drank my soul the light.

   Guest from the skies,
What is thy mission with the human heart?
   Sure Paradise
Claims priceless boons, where thou dost take a part.

   "Read on my brow
The branded covenant. To all men, peace.
   Ever from now
Let envy, jealousy, and all sin cease.

"In charity
Be to the souls of men as God to thee.
Eternity
Brings not a recompense more gratefully.

"When erring powers
Bind to the trembling flesh the piercing thorn,
Like trampled flowers,
Let sweeter incense on the air be borne.

"Learn to forgive
The wanton hand outstretched to grasp thy joys.
This 'tis to live,
Keep thyself free from all earth's gross alloys."

Spirit of love,
Speed swiftly on thy heaven-appointed way,
Till bright above
Beams the glad dawning of a better day.

R. P. Journal, 1872.

OUR MOLLIE.

Large and dark as a gazelle's
Are her eyes, with witching spells,
And her teeth are white as pearls,
And of all the little girls
    That we know,
  Our Mollie is the sweetest;
    That is so.

Could you hear her silvery voice
Trill the music of her choice,
Could you see her dimpled smile
Ripples o'er her face beguile,
    You would know,
  Our Mollie is the sweetest;
    That is so.

Could you watch her busy hands,
Working out their thousand plans,

And her feet, whose restive spells
Fall like water over shells,
> You would know,
> Our Mollie is the sweetest;
> That is so.

Could you kiss her rosy lips,
Which no others can eclipse,
You would know, with great or small,
She's the darling of them all;
> You would know,
> Our Mollie is the sweetest;
> That is so.

To Miss Mollie Kussner,
> Terre Haute, Indiana.
Music by L. Kussner.

LINES

Written while waiting on some business in the office of U. S. MARSHAL POOL, and where were also MESSRS. LOVETT, TEAR, and WORTH.

I'M many favors overdue,
    And grateful yet may prove it,
They still may find that proverb true,
    Who trust the good and Lovett.

May Mercy's Tear direct the rule
    Where modest Worth so still is,
For-oft above the placid Pool,
    Exhale the fairest lilies.

HOME MEMORIES.*

An exile, far from home and friends,
    I sought the busy street,
To chase from memory's tearful page,
    Home recollections sweet.
Along the crowded thoroughfare
    My idle footsteps strayed ;
A band of strolling minstrels passed ;
    I listened as they played

* Melbourne, Australia, 1885.

    Lonely and homesick, a stranger, I started out from my hotel, soon after arriving at Melbourne, for a walk, and in a few moments came upon a band of minstrels who were playing the familiar airs from the Bohemian Girl—favorite airs my daughter Evangeline used to sing so well while on the operatic stage. The music intensified my sadness, and returning to my room, the song suggested itself to me, and was at once written out. To convey the desired impression, the music which accompanies the respective words copied with each verse should be played from the beginning of the verse, and the two lines written after each interlude should be softly sung and repeated if desired.—A. L. B.

HOME MEMORIES.

Those dear, familiar songs of home,
    The songs of other years,
When her sweet voice in plaintive tones,
    The heart awoke to tears,
With songs that voice no more will sing
    My sadness to dispel.
This tender strain the harp-strings swept,
    And swept my heart as well :

        [Instrumental interlude.]

("I also dreamt, which pleased me most,
    That you loved me still the same.")

And as the music rose and fell
    And softly died away,
My heart went trembling back again ;
    Her soft white fingers play
Upon my heart, as o'er the keys
    She played, to comfort me,
The songs we loved in other lands,
    Beyond the tropic sea.
And ere the last note died away
    In numbers soft and low,

The vibrant chords another woke
  In tuneful overflow ;
And down the strings the minstrel's hand
  Swept lightly o'er again,
As softly woke the quivering chords
  In this pathetic strain :

[Instrumental interlude.]

("Of days that have as happy been,
  And you'll remember me.")

And yet again that tuneful hand
  The chord's new echoes woke,
Till overfull one slender thread,
  Of its own sadness broke !
And still above that severed cord
  The hand kept playing on,
As o'er the heart's rent chords again
  Life's rivers overrun.
And yet again the changeful lyre
  Kept on in numbers sweet,
Till over-sad with memory's thoughts,
  I hurried down the street.

While her sweet face led on before
    With songs she used to sing,
Thus played the hand upon the harp
    Above the broken string:

        [Instrumental interlude.]

("But memory is the only friend
    That grief can call its own.")

NUMBER FORTY-FOUR.

The rain was dripping drearily from roof to muddy street,
With muffled tread the sentry kept his lonely, solemn beat.
It was midnight. In the hospital the lamps were burning low,
And on the walls, fantastic, flung their shadows to and fro.

And every ward was crowded, with its hundred men and more,
For the winter's scourge had left them when the troops went on before;
When the fever and miasma, with their pestilential breath,
Stalked beside lagoons and bayous in the cerements of death.

And a painful sense of silence crept along the cheerless halls,
Broken only by the echoes where delirium's specter calls,

The moaning, and the hollow cough, or prayers' unconscious said,
The footfall of the night-watch or the nurse's slippered tread.

Sleep's gentle hand in fitful rest elixir's solace brought,
And on the fevered lids of some, forgetfulness had wrought.
And back in dreams the homesick boy through orchards seemed to roam,
And muttered oft to phantom shapes endearing words of home.

There was dearth of woman's tenderness and less of woman's tears,
For women weep their tears at home, while men break hearts with wars,
Save now and then in ministry, with home and friends forgot,
Her loyalty the patriot gave beside the sufferer's cot.

For weeks the wasting tooth of pain, relentlessly as fate,
Had claimed the little drummer, from a loyal Northern state.

The boys had named him "Baby, all the way from
    Illinoy,"
But the nurse, with woman's tactics, called him "some
    one's darling boy."

As his restless little fingers thinner grew from day to day,
He would tell her in his prattle of his home so far away;
Of his pony, and his phaeton, of his colt, his skates, and
    sled.
"When the Surgeon gives me furlough, I'll get well, I
    know," he said.

Then abrupt the story ended : " Lady, something in your
    eye,
Tells me—yes, I know it—that you think I'm going to
    die."
Then she made his pillow softer, stroked his little golden
    head.
"But our dear brave little soldier does not fear to die ?"
    she said.

"Only—could I see my sister—mother—she is gone, you
    know,—
And my father—and my brother,—maybe just before I go.

You will kiss me for my kin-folks—so the way I'm going now,
Won't seem quite so strange and lonesome,—like there's some one near I know."

Then he planned a distribution of his little wealth at home,
And the trinkets in his knapsack, of a boy's well treasured sum.
"Hardly know just where I'm going to—and if you wouldn't mind,
And read a chapter in the Book, I would think it very kind."

Then he drew his little Bible from beneath his pillow white,
And she held his hands, and talked a while, then down the hour of night
She led him with the prodigal whose wayward pilgrim feet,
Repentant, in the Father's house found welcome and retreat.

When at last she closed the chapter, peace on his brow reposed,
And to those eager eyes, afar, some glory seemed disclosed.

And o'er the trembling purple lips she bent to catch the word—
"And I—go—to my—mother," was the whisper that she heard.

Then she closed and kissed his eyelids, and a ring of golden hair
From his boyish tresses severed, for a weeping sister's care.
When morning flung the sunlight through the window, on the floor,
Another cot was empty. It was number Forty-Four.

MAJOR PAULINE CUSHMAN.

In Memoriam.

[Read by the author at the funeral.]

CALM, peaceful at last, like the breast of the river,
    When torrent and tempest and tumult are past,
When the cataract's thunder is silent forever,
    When storm-spent and placid and quiet at last,
When the rock-fretted rapids no longer are sighted,
    Reposeful, it reaches its furthermost shore,
And the lamplights of evening in Starland are lighted,
    And the travail and toil of the day are no more,—

She quietly sleeps, who was tossed on life's ocean,
    On whose wild waves of impulse her life-bark was borne
O'er the red fields of carnage and cannons' commotion
    Through the winds of adversity shattered and torn,
With a patriot's fire on her soul's altar burning,
    And a loyal heart's love that her faults should atone,
With a soul full of tenderness spent—unreturning—
    Neglected, forsaken, and dying alone.

Oh, fling not reproach at the last, when death's finger
    And seal on her lips and her heart-throbs are set,
On one who so loved with the children to linger,
    Whose innocent prattles she could not forget.
Ah me! it were better each comrade and woman
    Should ask of himself—were his own weakness known,
He could say to his conscience:—"I am better than human,
    That he, being sinless, should cast the first stone"?

O loyal heart, faithful heart, heroine, soldier;
    Breveted by Lincoln, by Garfield installed,
With the comrades in arms who went shoulder to shoulder,
    Imprisoned and captive, but never appalled.
For country and freedom, and the stars of "Old Glory,"
    Oh, let it drape over her, silent and dead,
For what more befitting her life's hallowed story
    Than forever its folds should unfurl o'er her head.

And we should regret, if regrets were availing,
    That we gave not the living these tributes of ours,
And crowned her with laurels, whatever her failing,
    And strewed o'er her pathway love's beautiful flowers;

And perhaps—who shall say that her lingering spirit
    Speeds happier on in its star-fretted way
That at last, and in death, we remembered her merit,
    And bless, as we honor, her record to-day?

Where softly she sleeps will the grave grasses quiver,
    When the west wind sweeps in from far over the sea;
In her dream she will float on that mystical river
    Where the palm trees of Aiden droop low o'er the lea,
And her bark will cast anchor among the pale islands,
    And the hands of the angels are beckoning near,
And the morning light dawns o'er the crest of the highlands,
    And an escort in armor to meet her appear.

And there on the banks of the river they cluster,
    At the call of the bugle they form into line,
And a glorified army death only could muster,
    And a national memory only enshrine.
She has gone! and among them on history's pages,
    When ours are forgotten, our children will tell
Of her deeds. And her name will live on through the ages.
    Pass on, O freed spirit, pass on, and farewell.

THE "LITTLE MATRON'S" GREETING

TO THE BOYS OF THE THIRTY-SECOND REGIMENT WISCONSIN VOLUNTEERS, IN REUNION AT RIPON, WIS., JUNE 27–29, 1893.*

Please call my name out, comrade. What is it that you
    say?
I'm not upon the muster roll? that I'm not here to-day?
Where have I been to since the war? Why, I've been
    'most everywhere,
But I've always been with you, boys,—won't someone
    answer "here"?

You may have quite forgotten, boys, while journeying
    down the years,
Full many a scene which in my heart some memory still
    reveres,

---

* I was appointed Matron and Nurse of the 32d. Wis. Vols. Inf. by Surgeon General Wolcott, of Milwaukee, and was with them in the field until overtaken by sickness, after a very severe campaign during a protracted epidemic.

But I never shall forget you till my days on earth are reckoned,
And I still would be at roll-call in the dear old Thirty-Second.

I was with you up at Oshkosh, when first you went on drill,
And I nursed you in the barracks when you swallowed your first pill,
And when below at Memphis, when with mud half overflowed,
You came in from the Pigeon roost, that execrable road.

And I can well remember, without trying very hard,
How we gathered in the sick ones at the Memphis Navy Yard ;
You were grimed and sick with fever, and so many were laid low,
Who were fresh in manhood's vigor but a month or two ago.

And my heart was sick with pity, tho' you always thought it light,
And my tears were always coming, tho' I wept them out of sight,

And I felt the pain that racked you as I bent above your cot,
And I tried my best to cheer you, that the pain might be forgot.

For I knew the homesick longing for the loved ones far away
Was more wasting than the fever, and I tried to make you gay;
And I let you call me "mother," "sweetheart," anything you pleased,
Till your sinking courage rallied and the homesick was appeased.

But the hardest thing about it was, when everything was done,
To see the flickering life go out of some dear mother's son,
And they said it wasn't quite so hard to die with woman's care,
And it gave them satisfaction to have me with them there.

But you couldn't know the hunger that was in my heart the while,
For altho' my heart was breaking, for your sakes I'd sing and smile.

Did you know in Southern prisons that I had a soldier lad?
And I missed my babies' kisses, and I couldn't help be sad.

But I seemed to hear entreating from your mothers at
 their prayers,
"Father, let some angel woman give my suffering boy
 her care;"
And so, boys, I stayed beside you and I did my level best,
Tho' I never packed a knapsack—was a soldier with the
 rest.

And I've often thought it singular that neither near or far
Is a monument erected to the women of the war,
Tho' the country needed women just as much as boys in
 blue,
And I rather think they helped you bring "old glory"
 safely through.

I don't count much on honors, tho,' that come when one
 is dead;
Better that consideration that will help you get ahead;
Aftermath suits some conditions when you've plenty and
 at ease,
But the toiler in the treadmill can't waste time upon his
 knees.

And my pulses throb with thinking of the half I couldn't tell,
When we camped out there at Chelsea, you will all remember well ;
There was room enough and plenty, and the tents were new and neat,
And the mess had pork and beans enough and baker's bread to eat.

And the boys all looked so handsome on parade and all in line,
And with only slight exceptions everything out there was fine,
And the boys behaved so lovely (we had none but lovely men),
That the guard-house held a captive, for a change, but now and then.

And the boys policed the district, it was something nice to note,
Tho' we entertained the stranger,—bovine, swine, and friendly goat,—
Who when growing too familiar, without jury or defense,
Went the way of such transgressors, filled our plates at their expense.

And the hospital extended till we took and cared for all,
Tho' sometimes they numbered many who came up at surgeon's call;
And there's some who will remember every bed was clean and snug,
And the drink was so refreshing from the Matron's "big brown jug."

To the blessed Sanitary Uncle Sam owed many thanks
For the thousands that recruited from the ever thinning ranks,
For their glorious ministrations, freely given on every hand,
Helped the boys preserve the Union and bring freedom to the land.

How I foraged from a neighbor for the sick, you may have heard,
And gobbled up his strawberries, and he couldn't say a word,
With the picket-guard on duty; and while we picked away
We sang "'way down in Dixie," and remarked we'd come to stay.

And the contrabrands, how thick they were, Sam, Caroline, and Kate,
And Dave, Octave, and Charlie; and the melancholy fate
That befel our little Walker, who was everybody's pet,
In his soldier clothes, by far too large; I seem to see him yet.

And I wonder if the chaplain will recall it, when I say
I have not forgot the pudding that he made for his birthday;
Tho' he watched and boiled and punched it from morn till afternoon
It came out like soup with raisins, and we ate it with a spoon.

I remember I was frightened once when ordered to report,
In a peremptory manner, and the Colonel was the court;
And I wondered what delinquence, dereliction, or what not
Caused my summons so abruptly as I hurried to the spot.

Well! the guard an escort waiting held so innocent a pair—
They were women, and protested they had nothing anywhere

That was contraband, and plied me with persuasions that were bland,
And to save the guard the trouble I just took them into hand.

And they begged, caressed, entreated, that I wouldn't "make 'em strip,"
But I knew my little business and I wouldn't let them slip;
So I took their big horse-pistols they were smuggling through the line,
And every one was loaded, and they carried eight or nine.

And when the summer ended and the frost was everywhere
We went to church in numbers, tho' scarce to say a prayer;
Tho' the church of General Forrest for another use was meant,
The sick men in the basement seemed in every way content.

And we served the Lord in earnest, at least I thought so then,
By caring for the soldiers, who of slaves were making men;

And I slept up in the pulpit, where I really thought it worse
To give sanction to a rebel than protect an army nurse.

But I'd better not detain you, there's so many to be heard,
But I thought I'd fly to pieces if I couldn't say a word;
Tho' it's sort of second-handed, and it seems a little hard,
I will send my silent double, who will represent my card.

Tho' I'm with you, boys, in spirit, ghosts like mine don't walk, they say,
But I'd give ten years of penance to be with you all to-day,
Just to see your dear old faces, just to catch your honest smiles,
To be really there among you I would walk a hundred miles.

So my corporate can't be with you—perhaps it's just as well,
For what might happen otherwise, might not be best to tell;
Tho' I love the girls right royally, the girls you left behind,
They might misconstrue the impulse, if not generously inclined.

Yet I can't quite reconcile it you should meet without
　　me there,
And I've set my head to thinking how to take you un-
　　aware;
I myself am no magician, if some magic could be found—
Stay! perhaps I might by proxy greet and hug you all
　　around.

And remember, when you see it, just the trifle that I send*
Just to show the Thirty-Second has in me a loyal friend,
That the hand that wrought the token would its ministry
　　bestow
Just as freely to a soldier as in war times long ago.

And there's one thing pretty certain, when we're called
　　in grand review,
At that grand eternal muster, I shall not be far from you.
If there's one among you, comrades, who is doubtful of
　　his fate,
I'll persuade the good Saint Peter just to pass him through
　　the gate.

* The trifle sent was a cream satin banner upon which I had painted in oil colors the "Little Matron's" portrait, full size. Our Chaplain is now the Right Rev. Bishop Samuel Fallows of the Diocese of Illinois.

True, I know you've hardly missed me, but 'twould gratify my mind
If you'd give just one hurrah, boys, for the girl now left behind;
And I'd prize the silken token as a keepsake, just to say,
"See, my boys did not forget me—here's the badge they wore to-day."

And if any of you, comrades, should be drifted out my way,
I'd suggest you'd better call a halt, and pass the time of day;
I am loth to leave you, comrades, and my heart is breaking quite;
I'll be with you next reunion; heaven bless you all—good-night.

  Your "Little Matron," in loyal affection,

         ADDIE L. BALLOU.

SAN FRANCISCO, CALIFORNIA.

REPLY TO A LETTER REQUIRING EXTRA POSTAGE,

FROM A PUNNING CORRESPONDENT.

At taking hints
You make no stints,
Nor prove to compact fickle;
Which, willing done,
With spicy pun,
Deserves the extra nickel. *

Professor Peet,
I'm yours to treat,
But make me this confession:
A kindly lick
Of fate might stick
You fast to your profession.

* Five cents postage at that time.

I send you cheer,
And change for beer,
Much pleasure be afforded :
Forgive, forget,
That dreadful threat ;
Return and be rewarded.

THE TAIL OF A TOAD.

AN IMPROMPTU.

I have an old aunt from the city,
   She's a sort of a genius and crank ;
She tries to be funny and witty,
   But her jokes seem to me rather rank.

My aunt had a pet that she tended,
   She tethered him out by a string.
I hope she will not be offended,
   But I thought it a horrible thing.

My aunt gave him flies for his diet
   When her day's work of painting was done,
But the flies feed on him, and he's quiet,
   And his toes are turned up to the sun.

And that is the end of my story,
  For his bones bleach out there in the road.
It's no fable, like "Old Mother Morey,"
  But my aunt and her little horned toad.

For Ethel, by the said aunt.
  REDLANDS, CAL ,
    June, 1891.

HAIL TO THE HERO!*

All hail to the hero whose coming we wait,
  When the ship shall sail in from the turbulent sea;
Then harbor-locked safe by our own Golden Gate,
  Oh, warm be our welcome in honor of thee!

In all the far lands through these pilgrimage years,
  All nations have gloried to honor their guest;
But hearts never leaped with such pride and glad tears,
  Nor hands with such welcome his never have pressed.

For our hero is ours, and we cannot forget
  The arm that was strongest on perilous field,
When the sky of our nation with crimson was set,
  And carnage and death left their stain on our shield.

Then ring out such welcome, with cannon and bell,
  As never a hero returning has known;
And spangle the air with the breeze-lifting swell
  Of the flag he defended, for his land and our own.

* Arrival of Grant at San Francisco, Sept. 15, 1879.

Then welcome, thrice welcome! our veteran chief,
    We are all of us loyal in welcome to thee—
To the soldier whose sword brought the bondmen relief,
    Our ruler, when peace spread her wing o'er the free.

Then thunder, ye guns, and ring loudly, each bell,
    And, music, give voice o'er the restless sea foam,
And stars shimmer down from your banners and tell
    How proudly we welcome our conqueror home.

LOU'S CHRISTMAS GIFT.

'Twas the night before Christmas,
    And poor little Lou,
For the want of a stocking
    Hung up her old shoe;
It was worn out and ragged,
    It was rusty and old,
It let out the pink toes,
    And it let in the cold.

"I'll just play I am sleeping,"
    The little one said,
"And when Santa Claus comes
    And looks into my bed,
And don't see me stir,
    He'll fill up my shoe
With all the nice things
    For my mamma and Lou."

"Merry Christmas to mamma!"
 As jumping from bed
To the shoe by the chimney,
 The little one sped.
"Oh, Santa! what made you?
 Just see what he's done!
He's filled up my shoe
 Full of snow, just for fun.

"I think he was naughty,
 A little bit too,
For, mamma, he didn't
 Leave nothing for you.
But never mind, mamma!
 I'll kiss you—don't cry!
'Spect he couldn't bring
 What my ma couldn't buy."

NEW ORLEANS, LA., 1872.

THE COMING MAN.

A REPLY TO "SANS SOUCI."

"Sans Souci," pray, what did you mean,
    When you laid out that terrible plan
Of the "witching, bewitchingly sweet,"
    And the traps that they set for their man?
Your "girl of the period," mister,
    The one that's best fitted your mood,
Would take her own chances at wooing,
    She never would wait to be wooed.

That the world needs be "reformed"
    And governed by "better rules,"
Is a truth that may well be applied,
    Since its rulers are knaves or fools.
Conventions and Congresses now
    Are scarce but a babel of noise
And squabbles and party strife,
    Led on by the tipsy b'hoys.

Don't wonder they "dream of place
   And power," and " a better morn,"
And as to the fireside virtues,
   Well, to-day there is little to scorn.
And as for the noisy forum,
   They've not very far to rush,
And your grapevine's purple lustre,
   Is naught but a nightshade bush.

If our women were all Cornelias,
   And the men of the period wed.
Their children would be but monkeys,
   If they "aped" from the parent head.
Our old-fashioned men, oh, where are they?
   They are gone with the woodbine, to grass,
And the men of to-day haven't mettle
   Enough for a compound of brass.

Lucretias to-day are the women
   Who to keep up appearance, you know,
Must dress, paint, and flirt to be charming;
   Not a sensible thing should they know.
The one who should dare to know other

Than what you might teach to a goose,
  Is a creature of Amazon habits,
    And a target for small men's abuse.

I'll tell you, "Sans Souci," what I think,
    These men have quite envious grown,
That a woman should be independent,
    Since this world has so long been their own.
The coin she so merrily "jingles,"
    Her rights by the earning have gained,
She's not forced to wed for a keeping
    Or honors she never attained.

Alas for these wronged little creatures,
    These poor little masculine elves,
They measure the "strong-minded women"
    By what is left out of themselves.
It is just as well that he comes not,
    This "coming man," 'tis no use,
Since hearts may be won by love only,
    And not by the croak of a goose.

LOUISVILLE, KY., 1871.

DEAD IN HIS BED.

Only a man dead in his bed; that is all.
Stark, stiff, and rigid, white face to the wall.

Came out of yesterday, somewhere, to here.
Well, no; don't think he'd friends anywheres near.

Wanted employment, that's what he said;
No work to give him,—next thing he's dead.

What did he die of, sir? Can any one tell?
A fit did they think it was? Last night he was well.

Heart disease? Maybe. What was his name?
Don't know; didn't register, sir, when he came.

Laud'num, they said it was, there on the stand.
No, stranger; don't reckon he held a fair hand.

Suicide? Yes, that's what the Coroner said;
Scooped out was what put the thing in his head.

DEAD IN HIS BED.

Money? Guess not, sir. Why, he hadn't enough
To pay for this hole in the sod, of the stuff.

Friends, did you ask? Oh, yes! sometime or other;
Reckon, of course, the boy once had a mother.

Rather rough on him, pard; but where's it to end,
When you're panned out of cash, and can't count on a friend?

Down to the calaboose—that's where they took him;
Good enough place when a man's money's forsook him.

Fun'ral? Just you see that express at the corners!
County don't pay for no hearse, nor no mourners.

Well, stranger, you've got me! Can pray, if you will;
Rather late in the day, when a man's dead and still.

Strikes me it don't count, to this, under my spade;
And as for the rest of him—stranger, that's played.

No offence, sir; beg pardon. But strikes me as fair,
And a pretty sure way to get answer to prayer,

Better give a poor devil a lift while he's here,
Than wait till he's passed in his checks over there.

Oregon Statesman, SALEM, Oct. 1, 1874.

L'ENVOI.

Down Memory's shadowy aisle to-night
   There sweeps the train of bygone years;
As stars with shimmering train of light,
   An army of the heaven appears;
   While night dews shed their crystal tears,
      Each orient space
      Some long-loved face
Unvails to bless my lingering sight.

Down by each time-familiar lane
   My mother walks, as in those days
When we were boys. Ah! would again
   Our eyes could meet her tender gaze
   As they looked then their love and praise.
      The soft caress,
      Her finger's press,
Was solace for all grief or pain.

Down where the silence is so deep—
   My thoughts give echo ere I speak—

L'ENVOI.

They laid you when you fell asleep,
  With death's pale lilies on your cheek.
  You, best beloved, who were so meek,
    So placid seemed;
    As if you dreamed
Of secrets that the angels keep.

Down from your now abiding-place
  Is there no passageway to ours?
No window, where your sainted face
  May look from out your spirit's bowers,
  To cheer us on life's lonely hours?
    Is there no word
    That may be heard,
Peace-giving in its thrilling powers?

Down Time's tempestuous coast at last,
  When life's frail tent for me is furled,
When night my day shall overcast,
  When wrecked and out of being hurled,
  Will your sweet eyes, by love impearled,
    In welcome wait
    At Aiden's gate,
And find me room in your blest world?

Evening Post, SAN FRANCISCO, 1877.

TERRA AUSTRALIS.

(CENTENNIAL CANTATA.)

Hail! hail! and welcome, all ye lands,
    Far reaching over many seas!
Hail! fleet-winged ships from every strand,
    That trail your pennons on the breeze!
Bring hither from your fruits of toil,
    Your choicest industries and arts,
Invoke the genius of your skill,
    Bring bounteous from your treasure marts.

Chorus.

Hail! hail! and welcome from every fair land,
    From east and from west, to our land of the free,
We give you the clasp of fraternity's hand;
    All nations are one in the world's jubilee.

Your world is mighty, the sea is wide,
    The prophet Time for you has wrought

Empires strong, for hearts of pride,
    Wise in the lore by sages taught.
From breast of the old the new world springs.
    Flushed is her heart with veins of gold.
Forging metals, and toiler sings,
    We shall be great ere we are old.

Backward only a hundred years,
    Silently under the southern cross,
Waste was our land as futile tears,
    And gold was idle, and time was loss.
Speeds now the engine's polished steel,
    Where but the trail the savage pressed ;
And ships come in, with sail and wheel ;
    Lightning and steam keep pace abreast.

Cities arise, mankind to bless,
    Over the waste of the years now gone ;
And church, and school, and printing-press
    Herald the light of a better dawn.
The children's hearts are light with song,
    And peace and plenty and joy abound,
The sinews that gird the state are strong,
    And toil is monarch the new world round.

Our herded hills and vales combine,
    And gardens honied sweet with bees,
And vintages o'errun with wine,
    And golden sands between our seas,
To give you welcome, far and wide
    Welcome! Excelsior, Gloria!
Be honored still with gracious pride,
    Country and queen, Victoria.

CHORUS.

MELBOURNE, VICTORIA, 1889,

WHICH DO YOU CHOOSE TO WEAR?

Which do you choose to wear, dear girl,
   The rose or the laurel? For both are fair.
The rose is for love, the laurel fame ;
   Whichever shall crown your shining hair?
Which shall the soul of your young life claim ?
   Which do you choose to wear, dear girl ?

Which do you choose to wear, dear girl ?
   Sweet with the breath of love is the rose ;
Under the rose is hid the thorn ;
   Queen of the hedge it lowly grows :
On the glacial heights is the laurel born.
   Which do you choose to wear, dear girl ?

Warm is the breath of the rose, dear girl ;
   Thorny the stem on which it grows.
Daisies above her grave may bloom,
   Over the laurel the cold wind blows,
Marble the walls of her final tomb.
   Which do you choose to wear, dear girl ?

Wear as you choose to wear, dear girl;
May they both entwine for you alway,
Laurel and rose, for love and fame;
Above your brows the evergreen bay,
And love be your heart's sweet oriflamme,
Is the prayer of my heart for you, dear girl.

To Miss Lena Boucicault, daughter of Dion Boucicault.
Steamer Zealandia, mid-ocean, June 21, 1883.

ACROSTIC ON A BLOTTER.

CHRISTMAS.

Says I to myself, 'Tis the last of the year,
  And I wish you much joy of the past.
Merry Christmas be with you and all its good cheer
  (Thank goodness it's with us at last).

Have a care for the new year, invoke the good saints
  Our fortunes and joys to increase.
Right the wrongs of the millions, unfetter restraints
  So let us have plenty and peace.

(On Cover.)

  As snow-flakes cover what autumn sears,
  So I blot out the inky tears.

TO ARMS!

Oh! sad were the tidings that reached us to-day.
Each flag at its masthead was fluttering gay,
But hearts hushed their beatings, and cheeks paler grew,
As the terrible story from lip to lip flew:
"Colonel Ellsworth is fallen, the pride of the braves,
The gallant young chief of the bold 'Fire Zouaves'."

A shadow of gloom o'er the busy town passed,
And the star-begemmed tricolors trailed at half-mast.
Long the nation will mourn that her hero should die
By a murderous hand, when no battle was nigh,
As fell Colonel Ellsworth, the pride of the braves,
The gallant young chief of the bold "Fire Zouaves."

His blood calls for vengeance, and thousands to-day
Are waiting the summons in battle array,
To strike for his downfall with vigorous hand,
And the flag that waves over our glorious land,
To avenge Colonel Ellsworth, the pride of the braves,
The gallant young chief of the bold "Fire Zouaves."

Chilton Republican, MENASHA, WIS., May 25, 1861.

SONG OF VICTORY.

We've touched the apex of our hopes!
   No longer woman pleading kneels,
To ask her heaven-appointed rights
   Of man, in tearful scorned appeals,
For backward now those doors have swung,
   That never opened but to men.
Her voice, once heard in Congress halls,
   Shall wake its corridors again.

Be patient, O ye pauper poor,
   And weary workmen at your desk,
Ye cringing menials in the dust,
   Your wrongs are soon to be redressed.
Ye servers on time-honored powers,
   A nobler power shall sway than kings;
No longer man shall despot rule,
   When woman's standard upward flings.

Wait, gloriously, ye crucified
  Of womankind, for come it must,
The day when you no more shall be
  A victim to man's selfish lust.
Up, then! to action, women, men,
  Nor longer wait in sluggish fear,
The right by vigilance shall win,
  And crowns of equal justice bear.

WASHINGTON, D. C., during the Woman's Suffrage campaign, Jan., 1872.

IN MEMORIAM.

(MEMORIAL DAY, SEVEN PINES CIRCLE,

LADIES OF THE G. A. R.)

(An Impromptu.)

OH ! my sisters, while memory lingers
   With the heroes who honored the blue,
While twining with tenderest fingers,
   The blooms o'er their graves to bestrew,
In the web of their love wreathing beauty,
   Inwrought for the deeds of the brave,
Who followed the stern call of duty,
   And sleep in a patriot's grave.

Forget not the tireless devotion,
   Of mother and sister and wife,
Whose love through the deadly commotion,
   Sustained those arrayed in the strife.

Their names are unwritten in story,
    The battles they fought are unsung,
No history heralds their glory,
    No wreath on their monument's hung.

Their hearts were a-hungered with waiting
    The scourge of the war to pass by;
With vigils that knew no abating,
    And a faith that was royal and high,
With tears, while their babes closer pressing,
    They bade them go honor the shield,
Till the wrongs of the nation redressing,
    With victory covered the field.

With a love that was all unrepining,
    And a loyalty true as the stars,
To the despot of fate all resigning,
    Bereft by the saddest of wars;
And the ruin and storms and confusion,
    The whirlwind of terrible shocks,
Have crimsoned life's peaceful illusion,
    And silvered the sheen of their locks.

And those who lie silently sleeping,
   Those sisters beloved of ours,
In faith to their loyalty keeping,
   We'll garland with memory's flowers.
And out from the heart of their petals,
   Shall gleam the white star of our love,
As the crucible holding the metals
   Reflects the pale light from above.

SAN FRANCISCO, May 23, 1892.

DADA'S MAN.

(GRANDBABY'S PRATTLE.)

No! grandma, I don't fink I can
Be your boy, 'cause I's a man,
My ma says, an' guess she knows;
Next year goin' to wear man's clo'es.

I works hard mos' every day,
Nen sometimes I has to play.
Sister ain't so big, like Roy;
Guess she wish she be a boy.

No! I ain't not 'fraid a bit;
Des hol's on an' rides old Kit,
Right up steep to dada's mine,
'Way up by the sugar-pine.

Mussent touch the poison-noak,
'Skeeters they don't like the smoke;
Lizard crawls up by eh trough,
Hit 'em, nen his tail drop off.

DADA'S MAN.

I puts ore-dirt in eh dump,
Rolls it down to hear it bump.
'Raster grinds it awful slow,
Nen I makes more water go.

I goes fru eh garden gate,
'Cos I has to irrigate;
Picks up acorns for eh pigs,
An' pine nuts; but *I* eats eh figs.

Yeller jackets sting me so
I fall down. Nen my ma fro
Water on me quick's she can,
'N I swell up mos' big's a man.

Mooley cow went to eh shop,
'Cos I couldn't make her stop.
Bonnie, he des bark en run.
Oh! we des had lots of fun.

Dada hold me pretty tight,
En we ride en ride all night
In eh steam-car to see you.
Street cars they des awful too.

Mamma says must hug you so,
'Cos she says she couldn't go.
'Course Roy 'll love you much's he can,
But he must be dada's man.

 Xmas, 1891.

SLEEP ON.

Sleep on, dear promise of Love's dream,
    I would not wake thy dreamless sleep;
Thy deathless spirit journeyed on,
    And I, alone, must wait and weep.
        Sleep on, sleep on!

Sleep on, sweet angel of my life,
    No mortal cares disturb thy rest;
Night's gentle zephyrs stir among
    The daisies growing o'er thy breast.
        Sleep on, sleep on!

Sleep on, in silent slumber sleep;
    I listen, but your voice is still,
And yet I hear love's vocal sound
    In silence, when I listen well.
        Sleep on, sleep on!

Sleep on, I would not bid thee wake
   To fill the weak cup of my life.
You were my all ; and art thou less
   My angel now, that wert my wife?
     Sleep on, sleep on !

Sleep on ; as pales the morning star,
   So passed away thy life and breath,
To light my night in life's decline.
   Death is not sleep ; yours is not death.
     Sleep on, sleep on !

AUTOGRAPH LINES.

(J. E. C.)

What shall I ask, to your life a boon?
Not that it be like an endless June;
Though of the rose 'tis the natal morn,
Still nurtured beneath is the hidden thorn.

Violets grow from the quickened earth,
Meek, like forgiveness and modest worth;
And these are May's, but an April's tears
Have sent her the floral crown she wears.

September is freighted with golden grain;
Her sunlight and even her harvest rain
Ripen the germs of the buds of spring,
And a halo of use over beauty fling.

Thus may your life like the autumn be,
From blasts of winter and storms quite free,
But enough of sunshine, enough of tears,
To span with the rainbow your arch of years.

Chagrin Falls, Ohio, Dec, 1866.

A MI QUIERIDO!

DARLING! each day with its resplendent wing,
    Infolds you closer to my yearning breast,
As tender pinions o'er the loved one cling,
    To clasp the new fledged birdling to its nest.

When you are near me, does the great black swell,
    That wrecked the past, its raging tumult cease?
Some tranquil whisper tells me all is well,
    And floods my soul in an impassioned peace.

So long my heart had starved, and loved in vain,
    I could not see the sunlight, for my tears;
To trust and love you, I forget my pain,
    And kiss your hands above the broken years.

Too much I trust the honor of your thought,
    To let my lips betray my heart's whole quest;
For, if you love me, or you love me not,
    Yours will divine, and give to mine the test.

MELBOURNE, VICTORIA, Oct., 1885.

PERDITA.

One night, a hurrying angel, filled with pity,
Heard a low infant's wail within the city;
She paused, her warm heart in her bosom throbbing;
Beside a door-stone knelt a mother, sobbing.

"Oh, pitying angel! let me for my sin so sorrow.
Hence from my breast, my babe,—if but to-morrow
Shall love and shelter her!—while, loveless and alone,
My broken heart can for such sin atone."

The angel stooped and, filled with pity, kissed her.
"Go, sin no more,—though frail, thou art my sister."
The door swung inward, and far streamed the light;
The babe with other angels nestled safe that night.

Terre Haute, Indiana, Oct., 1889.

BE RECONCILED.

(A RESPONSE TO RICHARD REALF, POET AND JOURNALIST.)

May the wing of the peace-angel hover,
    Thy tempest-tossed bosom above,
For why should the breath of the lover,
    Sigh hot o'er the altar of love?

'Twere better its Ætna to smother,
    E'er reaching the noon of its height,
Than gulf the wrecked life of another,
    In the furious sea of its blight.

For love is not love, if unmated;
    It survives but in oneness alone;
And to death must that bosom be fated,
    That is always bereft of its own.

SAN FRANCISCO, July 3, 1878.

A FRAGMENT.

I do not mind that the good-night words
    With lingering fondness were once unspoken,
That the tender touch of a good-night kiss
    Gave not to my lips the accustomed token.

I do not mind all the weary hours,
    Which the lonely vigils deprived of sleeping,
Though a throbbing head and a beating heart
    The sentinel watch to the night are keeping.

I only grieve that a heart so loved
    Should prize so lightly love's priceless treasure
As to spill the wine with a careless hand,
    And break with neglect its crystal measure.

PORTLAND, OREGON, November, 1878.
  The City Argus, San Francisco, Cal.

OUR BABY.

(To music by Felix Schelling, Philadelphia, Pa.)

BEAUTIFUL humming-bird, sipping the flowers,
    Robbing their cups of their delicate sweets;
Dear little golden-haired birdling of ours,
    Pattering soft with her little bare feet.

Dear little mocking-bird, all the long day
    Saying the baby words scarce understood,
Catching the flecks of the sunlight at play—
    Ah! she would catch the great sun if she could.

Cuddles her tired head cosy for sleep,
    Watching the moon and the stars in the sky;
Softly the dimpled arms round my neck creep,
    Lisping to "mamma" her "lullaby-by."

Sleep, little innocent, little "Bo-peep!"
    Come never over her shadow, but sheen;
Angels protect her, awake or asleep,
    Golden-haired slumberer, Evangeline.

YOUR PRAISE.

THAT night when the crowd applauded much,
    When the house was filled and I did my best,
I eagerly watched if I could but touch
    Your heart in response with all the rest;
You paid me the homage of your praise,
    In a reverent touch to my lifted brow,
Your proud eyes lent their approving rays,
    But you said me good-night with a formal bow.

Last night when the crowd was far the less,
    And a wearisome pain convulsed my frame,
Though never a one could my agony guess,
    Your eye flung o'er me its tender flame.
Because I faltered, you praised the more;
    Like a child you drew me to your warm breast,
As you never had held me there before,
    And your good-night kiss to my lips you pressed.

August, 1878.

OH, WHERE ARE THE LITTLE BOYS?

The house is so empty, so lonely and still;
   The embers are fitfully dying;
The wintry tears fall on my window-sill,
   And my heart keeps sobbing and sighing
     For the little boys that were lent to me,
     In the long ago, by the inland sea,
     Where birds, and blossoms, and winds were free.

For back again were my little boys
   Last night, in reality seeming;
And all the old pride and motherly joys
   Were mine through the bliss of dreaming
     Of the little boys with their bare brown feet,
     With their milk-white teeth and breaths more sweet
     Than the clover blooms where the honey-bees meet.

Two tangled webs of the softest brown,
  Like bronze into amber molten ;
And one with ringlets of flaxen down,
  Reflecting the sunlight golden.
    And sweeter than song of any bird
    That ever the woodland echoes stirred,
    Was the music of even their slightest word.

One slipped life's sandals whose baby song
  First lisped in the voice of an angel ;
Since my arms enclasped him it seems so long,
  Twin-born and my life's evangel.
    No shadow of earth his purity mars,
    Who waits by the gate whose golden bars
    Exceed the limit of countless stars.

What would I give if their broken toys
  Were about me, all order defying,
And the silken heads of my little boys
  Were asleep on their pillows lying ?
    For the perfumed kiss of their baby lips?
    My breast so yearns for their finger-tips
    To fling o'er life's shadows love's sweet eclipse.

They are all far away, my boys that are men;
  None ever were nobler or better;
They bless me through each happy stroke of the p
  Through each "dear little mother's" letter.
    Why should I grieve if a fairer face,
    With its youthful glow and a sweeter grace,
    In the heart of my boys holds dearer place?

Perhaps my boys will come back again,
  And my heart be at rest from its roaming,
When the little boys of my boys that are men,
  Shall be stars to my day in its gloaming.
    For who knows but ere my heart grows cold,
    As my head grows silvered above the gold,
    Their baby boys shall my arms enfold?

SAN FRANCISCO, CAL., April, 1879.

OPEN THE BLIND.

SERENADE.

The moonbeams lie white on the rose-bush and lawn,
The night is fast passing, it soon will be dawn.
Oh! wake from your pillow, bid slumber be gone,
   Throw open your casement, O beautiful maid!
The sky's bending o'er you, while stars, gleaming bright,
Like eyes of the angels that watch you by night,
Are calling you, love; and the moon's silver light
   A shimmering glance on your window has laid.
      Open the blind, love, open the blind;
      Open the blind, love; tender and kind
      Blows the soft breath of the summer-warm wind;
      Star eyes are watching, love, open the blind.

Oh, lady, awake! do the stars vainly wait?
The moon will not tarry, she answers 'tis late;
And long has the night-birdling crooned to his mate;
   The river is kissing the lips of its shore,

Imploring, in ripples that sparkle and dance,
My star-eyed to fling them her rivaling glance.
Then, lady, awake! let thy presence enhance
   The beauty of earth, and the heaven bending o'er.
      Open the blind, love, open the blind;
      Open the blind, love; tender and kind
      Blows the soft breath of the summer-warm wind
      Star eyes are watching, love, open the blind.

Then open your window, for tender and true,
As the heart of the rose that is kissed by the dew,
The heart that is calling is beating for you,
   Is calling you, love, to awake from your sleep.
As pure is her heart as the snow on the breast
Of the snowiest mount, on the loftiest crest.
In sleep or awake may she ever be blest.
   Thy vigils above her, oh! peace, angels, keep!
      Open the blind, love, open the blind;
      Open the blind, love; tender and kind
      Blows the soft breath of the summer-warm wind
      Star eyes are watching, love, open the blind.

PORTLAND, OREGON, August, 1878.

AUTOGRAPH LINES.

(ALBUM, MISS GRACE E————.)

As happy as your dreaming,
As fair as summer seeming,
With blessed joy be teeming,
    The future of your years.
And when your heart is mated,
May love be ne'er abated,
To joy, your wifehood fated,
    And know no vale of tears.

TURLOCK, CALIFORNIA, Dec. 1884.

HER LETTER.

My Darling:

Three days have lifted their glory above you,
Since I answered you, Yes, dear heart, I love you.

Three days, and they should have been weeks instead,
By the busy thoughts that have throbbed in this head.

Three crooked days, with their worse and better,
And "I love you" can only be spoken by letter.

And pray, dear, what must you think of the sphinx
Who sketches her cupids with pen-points and inks?

For, darling, "I love you" falls short of its bliss,
When letter seals steal the sweet seal of a kiss.

And, sweetheart, "I love you" is sweetest when told
By every sweet art which love's secrets unfold.

Then how can I lift to your lips love's full bowl,
And in word crystals flash the full light of the soul?

And, darling, what if I love you as deep
As the limitless depths where the thunders sleep?

If my heart like the steel in its sheath were as set,
And you were the gem-studded hilt's silver fret?

What if you were the sunlight's meridian glow,
That could melt into rivers my life's ice and snow?

What then? If the child were so loyally true,
Would a constant "I love you" be echoed by you?

And true as the stars that watch nightly above her,
Would you be to such love an unfaltering lover?

Would you open your bosom the doveling to nest,
And say to the weary heart, Come here and rest?

Would you sometime grow weary of too much caressing,
And prize not the love that lives only in blessing?

Would you not, as a dreamer who shakes off his dreams,
Fling her from your life with day's ruddier gleams?

Oh! tell me, I'm eagerly waiting to know,
How you'll shelter my birdling with pinions of snow.

Impatient to break this bewildering spell,—
If you love me, my darling, write quickly and tell.

For darling, I love you, I love you—what then?
May angels protect you; God bless you; amen!

SACRAMENTO, CAL., May, 1874.

COLUMBIA.

Loveliest stream among the rivers,
   In the northland's lakelets born,
Where the glacial mountain shivers
   Through the wintry summer morn ;
Where no foot of man or maiden
   Other than the duskier-hued,
Treads the wilderness, o'erladen
   With its wildest beast or brood.

Hurrying on, nor ever staying—
   Why so swiftly through thy Dalles?
Coyly, with the shadows playing,
   Madly, where the cascade falls ;
Placid now, but yonder flirting
   With the sunset, crimson-dipped,
Where the hills the west is skirting,
   Passion-hued in blushes tipped.

Through the rocky cañons falling,
    Shimmering, laughing, to the sea,
To the stars coquetting, calling
    "Fling your mantle over me;"
To the snow mount, "Do you miss me
    From your summer melting height?"
To the moon, "Oh, come and kiss me,
    Sparkle on my breast to-night."

On forever, wondrous river,
    Will you never pause nor rest?
Will you cease from hurrying, never,
    Till upon the ocean's breast?
Vainly strive the shores to hold you,
    Stay, O river, you are lost
Once the Ocean's arms enfold you,
    Where the tides are tempest-tossed.

But her sandal ribbons tinkle
    Into loops and girdling sheen,
Broadening in her skirts to twinkle
    On the fir's reflected green.

"Let me go to meet my lover,
    Golden treasures wreathe my way,"
Thus she sings, while sails above her
    Bear her golden sweets away.

And the passion-spuming ocean,
    With his lips all foaming white,
Rushes to her with commotion,
    "You shall be my bride to-night,"
Kneels upon the shore to lave her,
    Frantic leaps the stranding bar.
"She is mine, no power can save her!"
    Shrieks o'er sail and plunging spar.

THE DALLES, Sept. 4, 1878.

SINCE MOTHER DIED.

Oh, memories sweet of my childhood's home,
  Swiftly ye glide o'er the waves of time;
    Again I sit with the loved ones there,
    And mother is still in the dear old chair;
  Yet sad is the music of memory's chime
      Since mother died.
        Oh, mother!

My father loved in those golden days
  To lift the wee ones upon his knee;
    But his smile went out, leaving lines of care;
    The silvery threads have crept into his hair.
  Oh, bitterly sad is that home to me
      Since mother died.
        Oh, mother!

SINCE MOTHER DIED.

And where, oh, where are the cherished ones now?
    Four of our number have joined her there.
        One leads his braves in the cause of right,
        One comforts the dear old man to-night;
    Her babe, he has grown to a man of care .
            Since mother died.
              Oh, mother!

One pale and delicate all his youth,
    Now prospers well in his happy home;
        And one—she erred, but we love her yet,
        And the days of her innocence never forget,
    For we know how often the sorrows come
            Since mother died.
              Oh, mother!

And I—each hearth hath its wandering one—
    Ah, me! are the home-joys forever flown?
        Often I sigh for a kindred's love,
        And would fly to that ark like a fugitive dove;
    Yet why do I murmur—alone, alone,
            Since mother died?
              Oh, mother!

For oft when the shadows of twilight fling
  The breath of the evening upon my brow,
    Or the midnight hour, with its wild unrest,
    With throbbing brow to the pillow pressed,
I have felt the thrill of that voice so low
      Since mother died.
        Oh, mother!

O blessed light from the spirit's love,
  Hovering over to guide and cheer,
    How ye banish the terrors of life or death;
    Ah! they come again with the night wind's breath.
Welcome, dear forms that are ever near
      Since mother died.
        Oh, mother!

Banner Of Light, FOND DU LAC., WIS., 1864.

AFTER THE BATTLE.

One, the darling of a household, a widow's only son,
Was gathered with the wounded when the battlefield was won;
And a comrade bending o'er him smoothed his couch with manly care,
While the moon looked down in pity, glinting through his raven hair.

In his hand, so firm in battle, trembling lay a gilded case,
And the dying soldier's teardrops fell upon a pictured face.
Gory was the golden ringlet he so lovingly caressed,
Till the dying hand, grown weaker, let it fall upon his breast.

"Yes, I know it, Will, I'm dying; I shall soon be out of pain;
And the home and friends so dearly loved I shall never see again;

And I ask it as a comrade, if you should outlive the strife,
That you bear my last short message to my mother and my wife.

"Tell my mother to repress her tears, for the love she bears her son ;
There have many noble sons been slain that victory might be won ;
And although my life is going, and I know 'tis sweet to live,
What I now regret most deeply is, I have but one to give.

"Tell my sister I would give her some memento of my care—
Oh, I know how they will miss me from the old familiar chair—
Tell her to be brave, and tender of our mother's failing years ;
They will have to face the battle in life's field of bitter tears.

"Like the lave, she's pure and noble, she has ever been my pride,

AFTER THE BATTLE.

Than that I should fall in battle, she herself had sooner died.
Tell her, all the love she bore me she must give my fragile flower,
And the good all-seeing Father will reward life's darkest hour.

"You will go to that dear cottage where the prairie roses twine,
You will meet my own dear loved ones in the home that once was mine,
And my Mary—you will know her by this tress of golden hair,
And her cheek of lily whiteness, she was always frail and fair—

"Give her these—this case and ringlet, I shall never want them more;
I have never sunk in slumber but I've kissed them o'er and o'er.
She will not have long to mourn me; we shall meet full soon, I know;
She cannot face the bitter storms in this cold world of woe.

"Raise me—Will, I'm growing fainter; place your arm
    beneath my head—"
One upward glance, one sigh, a struggle, and the soldier's
    soul had fled;
And a light came o'er his features blending in a heavenly
    smile,
As if angel forms were waiting in the moonlight all the
    while.

Milwaukee Sentinel, June 11, 1862.

THE MANIAC'S LAST HOUR.

Dead ! dead ! and away from me?
　My darling cannot be dead !
Let me tear up this marble slab,
　And see if it cover her head.

Dead ! and is God dead too,
　That he heard not the cry of my heart,
To spare the dear life of my love,
　And to let not her spirit depart?

Dead ! and the sun is blood
　To my life, and the moon is out,
The stars are like serpent's eyes,
　That look on a heart of doubt.

Mad ! who said I was mad?
　How dare they to pinion me so?
Do they think to divide us by death?
　No, I'll sunder the earth but I'll go.

Fiends, back again to your den,
    And bring me the soul that has fled,
Or tear out my own heart, and fling
    In the waves of the sea of the dead.

Ha! ha! she is coming at last;
    She beckons me over the reef.
Just one leap into the dark;
    Down, walls, and give me relief.

Ha! So! now the crimson tide
    From my veins in a torrent starts.
Oh, where are the bolts and bars
    That can bind up such broken hearts?

I am coming, my love, to you,
    On a 'wildered and tempest-tossed wave;
One moment—how dark it grows!
    Ah! dying?—God pity and save.

INSOMNIA.

O Pilgrim Sleep ! O wanton god !
    Why leave so long my lids unkissed,
While Night, with silver sandal shod,
    Lifts her gray pinions in the east?
I saw thee linger by my door,
    And turn its latch, and sweetly smile,
When, lo ! a shadowy ghost before,
    Crept noiseless in and sat awhile.

"AND A LITTLE CHILD SHALL LEAD THEM."

I sat by the fireside dreaming
    Of hopes that had fled with the past;
Like the roses of youth they had perished,
    And left me a skeptic at last.

And I said, as I gazed on the embers
    That burned with a beautiful glow,
Till the flames in their upward leaping,
    Left only the ashes below:

As such is the life of a mortal,
    A torch for a moment of light,
To die like my beautiful embers,
    'Mid the shades of a rayless night.

Once mine, like the life that was glowing
    But a half hour ago in the grate,
Was warm with the love-light within me,
    And I knew not the meaning of fate.

Till now, with it constantly breaking,
  My heart has grown bitter and chill,
And philanthropy feeds the affections,
  And makes me a slave to my will.

And thus, like the glow of the embers,
  My life will go out by and by,
And I, like the ashes, forgotten,
  Shall crumble to dust where I lie.

When down through the deepening twilight,
  And soft on the evening air,
A voice that was near me whispered:
  "Of such have the angels care.

"As crushed is the vintage by pressure
  That yieldeth the choicest wine,
So hearts that have greater missions
  Are crushed by the hand divine."

Then the air seemed filled with music,
  And the clouds were drifted aside,
And I saw with the throng that entered,
  My beautiful boy that died.

And looking at me so fondly,
    With his eyes of the sky's own blue,
He said, " If God cares for the sparrow,
    Don't you think he will care for you?"

Then I prayed to the Father, Forgive me.
    Take not from my life its care,
But strength to my faint heart give me,
    Life's burdens the better to bear.

R. P. Journal, MANKATO, MINNESOTA, 1867.

TAKE COURAGE.

I've found in journeying up and down,
    Good yields, where'er you make it;
And who would wear a victor's crown,
    Must pave the way to take it.

While some would weakly wait for fate
    To set in fortune's favor,
I've found the wheel of fate decides
    For him whose stroke is braver.

When round and round the ceaseless waves
    Of opposition take you,
When one by one, like summer leaves,
    Your summer friends forsake you;

When doubtful hopes, like leaden skies,
    Hang heavily above you,
When treasure, golden phantom, flies,
    And leaves no heart to love you;

Don't be afraid, but lift your head,
    Let not despair assail you,
With earnest will and steady tread,
    Your purpose cannot fail you.

This world's not all a wanton waste,
    But interspersed with mountains,
And he who will may climb their crest,
    And taste their cooling fountains.

With ruddy health and honest heart,
    Just flout the grim dissenter,
When motive power the muscles start,
    Success ne'er failed a venture.

And Fortune's wheel continuous makes
    Her varied revolutions,
And never stays her well-poised stakes
    At half-formed resolutions.

Be brave your heart, your standard high,
    And never dare forsake it;
Your motto this, whate'er you try,
    "I'll find a way, or make it."

KNIGHTS OF PYTHIAS.

(ANNIVERSARY POEM.)

ANOTHER year Time's sifting sand
   Has gathered with his treasures;
O'er all the land, with bounteous hand,
   Swell nature's well-poised measures.
And in the virgin lap of spring,
   Of all the seasons sweetest,
Her buds she flings, and with them brings
   Hope's promise of completeness.

Again the ruddy cheek of May,
   With carnate blush diffusing,
With blossoms gay, trails in the day,
   While memory's page perusing,
Turns back to anniversaries fled,
   That fleck the gone forever;
Whose fragrance shed, above, tho' dead,
   Shall be forgotten never.

For genial seasons still will bring
    Their changes, sun o'er shadow ;
New birds will sing with each new spring,
    New grasses deck the meadow ;
And nature's story freshly told,
    Her goblet still renewing,
New threads of gold among the old
    She weaves with each reviewing.

So, smiling over winter's crest,
    She breaks his shivering lances,
And on the breast she loves the best,
    She flings her amorous glances ;
Till heaving with responsive dews,
    Lo ! earth with heart a-quiver,
With passion hues, the virgin wooes,
    To recompense the giver.

The courtly knights of olden days,
    Whose chivalry we honor,—
Not such bright days as these, our May's,
    With golden bars upon her,—
Saw in their festive time arise
    Nor half the shimmering splendor

As ours, whose skies reflect their dyes,
   In lingering sunsets tender.

For golden are our promised grains,
   That gather through their sluices;
The golden grains from earlier rains,
   And golden vintage juices,
Make promise, with maturing suns,
   Fruition for to-morrow;
From mountain runs, in golden tons,
   Our treasury we borrow.

And golden are the gates that bar
   The sea's pacific motion,
As from afar the wave-rocked spar
   Speeds o'er the waste of ocean;
And in our harbor land-locked lay
   The fleets from every nation—
From far Cathay, and ice-bound bay,
   From every sea-washed station.

To consecrate and weld anew
   The sacred ties of friendship,
Our Pythian love for Damon prove,
   Cement fraternal kinship,

Revive the errantry of knights,
    To kindly greet each other,
To reunite, and in our might
    To be to each a brother.

Thus do we celebrate the day
    Replete with most of gladness,
When blossoms play o'er each new way,
    And leave no room for sadness.
Thus do we press in friendship's palm
    Each hand, with clasp fraternal;
Through storm or calm, or rude alarm,
    Our kinship is eternal.

Long live the recompense of good,
    The price of honor's merit,
To those who, wooed by mercy, stood;
    Their strength may we inherit,
To lend sweet charity to all,
    Though erring footsteps lead them;
Wrong tempteth all, the strong may fall
    When storms enough impede them.

So down by Babylonian streams,
    Where sits the mourning weeper,

When early gleams—morn's tranquil beams—
  Send us like willing reaper,
Who gathers up the yellow sheaves,
  Bestowing to the gleaner,
Whose bounty leaves, to grant retrieves,
  To him whose lot is meaner.

We'll give benevolence indeed,
  To every cause that needs us;
We'll sow good seed, the hungry feed,
  Where tender pity leads us;
Where'er misfortune sends a blight,
  We'll give that cause assistance;
To every right we give our plight,
  To every wrong resistance.

Here each one labors to advance
  The honors of his station,
To so enhance his circumstance,
  And rise by acclamation.
The page, who, with the titled squire,
  On knighthood is attendant,
May still aspire to orders higher,
  Become the knight commandant.

Whoe'er his plume would graceful **wear,**
    Must plume himself by labor,
For none may share these honors **rare**
    Through merit of his neighbor.
As sturdy knights, in valor strong
    As ever lifted visor,
In deed or song to us belong,
    None happier nor wiser.

And as the labors of the years
    Put nature's crown upon her,
So he who bears our order's spears
    May win the spurs of honor.
To chivalry and valor when,
    Each loyal cause attending,
Indite we then by speech and pen,
    Be knighthood's day unending.

Nor shall the chivalry of knights
    Excel our impulse human,
We still indite, in love of right,
    The debt we owe to woman.
One toast we pledge, and that not long,
    O woman! ne'er forsake us!

Your virtues long we'll sing in song,
    We're only what you make us.

Then many blessings on the day,
    And to our noble order;
May each fair May like this be gay,
    Along time's fretted border.
May friendship, linked with charity,
    Benevolence bestowing,
Our watchword be, the future see
    The harvest of our sowing.

Read May 1st, 1878.

WELCOME TO GRANT! *

Dear General Grant, you are welcome at home,
   'Twould be hard to tell how we have missed you,
While you have been cradled on every sea's foam,
   And crowned heads have been vieing to feast you.
You have journeyed, no doubt, where the flowers are as sweet,
   Round the bowers of old knightly romances;
But the children would here cast them down at your feet
   As the hour of your coming advances.

How we eagerly watched for that last homeward trip,
   Till anxiety governed our senses;
And the shout that went up when they signalled the ship,
   Was heartfelt and free from pretenses.
Of course we are proud that they prize you abroad,
   And honors were each day repeating,
But none in those far-away lands you have trod,
   Could give you so hearty a greeting.

* Written for Camp-Fire and Reception, to U. S. Grant, Sept., 1879

or the "boys" who went with you at Abraham's call,
  When the land with disunion was shaken,
To defend or to die, that one star should not fall,
  Or its place on our shield be forsaken, —
The soldiers who shouldered their knapsacks to tramp
  Through the swamps and the poison morasses,
To picket at night far from shelter or camp,
  To guard all the dangerous passes, —

Their hearts are as loyal as when in the blue,
  They followed the fifer and drummer
In that line, the invincible order from you,
  Though it took the whole army all summer.
They honored in peace, and they loved you in war,
  No distance can memory sever;
All people may love you wherever you are,
  But the "boys" want you with them forever.

But isn't it grand that the war-cry is hushed,
  That crimson no more are the rivers,
And the cheek of fraternity no more is flushed
  With the hate that our unity severs,
That they who were bravest in battle array,
  And Roman-like went to defeat you,

The valorous boys who defended the gray,
    Side by side with the blue went to meet you?

They only remember the happier side,
    Appomattox and Lee's surrender,
Yet honor the soldier, with patriots' pride,
    As the country's most gallant defender.
And we know that the roll-call of honor above,
    Since Death on his bosom has laid them,
Leaves nought of the red on his signet, but love,
    And nought in our hearts to upbraid them.

And Washington, Abraham, Stonewall, and Lee
    Will still be the nation's evangels,
With all the brave souls from the land of the free,
    Whose muster has called to the angels,
Who loving the land of our banner have died,
    The tricolor's liberty bore us;
May nothing the stars in its azure divide,
    And forever one banner float o'er us.

GO AND TELL IT TO THE BEES.

O MY FATHER, A. H. HART, WHO PASSED AWAY AMONG HIS BEES, AT APPLETON, WIS, IN HIS 75TH YEAR.

    Have you heard the olden legend
      By the eastern people told,
    Of the sweet, strange superstition,
      That when Death's dark pinions fold
    Newly round some cherished loved one,
      Then the dearest friend to these
    To the busy hive must hasten,
      And must tell it to the bees?

    Is it true, some spirit lingers
      'Twixt their busy lives and ours,
    And that half their sweets they gather
      From the breaths of human flowers?
    Did some other winged thing tell them,
      When the bees, o'er drifts of snow,
    To her window came to perish,
      When she died, who loved them so?

How distinctly I remember
   All those drear un-mothered years;
Of the lake-side and the cottage
   Where I wept my childish tears;
How from early budding April,
   Till the autumn sered the trees,
Every twilight found my father
   Busy with his swarms of bees.

For they loved him and caressed him
   With their gauzy, restless wings,
Dusty with the yellow pollen,
   Girt about with golden rings.
Year by year they thus enriched him,
   With the sweets from flowering trees;
And with each white thread that crowned him,
   Dearer grew to him the bees.

Oh! I know how they will miss him
   All the summer afternoons,
When the languid perfume lingers
   O'er the lily-spread lagoons.
And the angel that received him
   Must have told among the trees,

When the dear old man, grown weary,
   Fell asleep among the bees.

Busy bees, cease not your humming,
   Burdened with the summer's sweets,
Hallowed thoughts round you are clustered,
   Where the past and future meets
When shall come the dark-winged angel,
   And my weary spirit frees,
Will some loving friend or kindred
   Tell it to my father's bees?

Appleton Press.

FOUR-LEAF CLOVER.

A FAIRY LEGEND FOR FOUR LITTLE DOTS.

Down the lane, up the lane, over and over,
Four little dots hunt the four-leaf clover.
Oh, queen-mother fairy, come out of the bell
Of the four-o'clock's ruby-red lip and tell
Where they grow. And she heard a little sob
From Lizzie and Nannie and Helen and Bob.

All day in the clover they vainly were trying
Four little leaves on a stem to be spying;
For who finds this clover needs only to wish,
To eat berries and cream from a pure silver dish.
The fairy queen came from a white lily bell,
And Baby Bob vanished, where no one could tell.

Down in the grass in a nook that was shady,
Searching again went each eager young lady.
"Fairy queen, fairy queen, where is our clover?"
"You shall learn, dots, when the searching is over."
From a pansy's heart danced the wee fairy queen,
And Helen and Nannie could nowhere be seen.

And Lizzie, the elder, a lone little rover,
Looked for Helen and Baby and Nan in the clover.
She called and she ran, and, oh! how she tried,
As she searched through the grass, till she sat down and cried.
The fairy's wand dropped with a soft, gentle sweep,
And the tired little darling fell fast, fast asleep.

The sunlight came up o'er the dear fairy mother,
And she knew how the little ones each loved the other.
She shook out the dew from her bright diadem,
And four leaves grew out on a soft little stem.
She named them, and guess the four names if you can;
They were Baby Bob, Lizzie, and Helen, and Nan.

SAN FRANCISCO.

GARFIELD.

Dead! He is dead, our beloved commander;
    Worn out at last, his proud spirit is free;
Promoted to orders still higher and grander
    Than those he laid down at the ebb of life's sea.
  Care for him tenderly, angels, who came for him;
  Noblest of earth's are the titles we claim for him,
  What more endearing in heaven will they name for him?

Vain were the prayers to restore to our numbers,
    Vain were our tears, but God best understands;
Restful at last he so peacefully slumbers,
    Safe in the keeping of holier hands.
  Care for him tenderly, angels, who came for him;
  Noblest of earth's are the titles we claim for him,
  What more endearing in heaven will they name for him?

Comrade and hero, all virtues combining,
    Soul all too pure for life's rancor and stain,
Suffering wrongs and all pains unrepining,
    Heart of the nation, in martyrdom slain.
  Care for him tenderly, angels, who came for him ;
  Noblest of earth's are the titles we claim for him,
  What more endearing in heaven will they name for him ?

Silent the tears of the nation are falling,
    With the grief-stricken mother's, whose tenderest care
Each hour some sweet thought of her boy was recalling,
    And devising new gifts for her hands to prepare.
  Care for him tenderly, angels, who came for him ;
  Noblest of earth's are the titles we claim for him,
  What more endearing in heaven will they name for him ?

And we weep for her heart who so bravely is bearing
    The grief that comes deepest to such widowed lives ;
The weeds that she wears the whole nation is wearing,
    And we honor and love her, the noblest of wives.
  Care for him tenderly, angels, who came for him ;
  Noblest of earth's are the titles we claim for him,
  What more endearing in heaven will they name for him ?

For the children, thrice blessed in a father so tender,
    Who will nevermore cluster in play at his knees,
Our prayers we unite to the orphan's defender;
    We are all of us orphaned in grieving with these.
Care for him tenderly, angels, who came for him;
Noblest of earth's are the titles we claim for him,
What more endearing in heaven will they name for him

O spirits of heroes whose deeds are immortal!
    O bosoms of Lincoln and Washington blest!
Infold and enshrine in your star-fretted portals
    Our belovèd commander, and give to him rest!
Care for him tenderly, angels, who came for him;
Noblest of earth's are the titles we claim for him,
What more endearing in heaven will they name for him
    Garfield, our comrade, beloved and blest!

SAN FRANCISCO, Sept. 22, 1881.

A CABIN HOME.*

On we go o'er vale and upland,
>   Fragrance fills the dewy morn,
Joyously we breathe the odors
>   From the meadows newly shorn.

Now we pass the rustic village,
>   Which so near the forest stands,
That it seems like hidden jewel
>   Girt about by emerald bands.

But farewell, dear quiet village,
>   Other haunts than thine we seek,
'Tis a cabin where the wild winds
>   Fan a budding maiden's cheek;

Where the graceful woodbine twineth
>   Sweetly by the cabin door,
And a breeze, ofttimes too playful,
>   Strews its blossoms o'er the floor;

---

* Written impromptu on visiting the home of General Benj. J. Sweet, in the suburbs of Chilton, Calumet Co., Wis., in June, 1862.

Where the noise of babbling children
    Echoes through the forest wild;
Was there ever music sweeter
    Than the dear voice of a child?

And the mother's voice of welcome,
    Can we e'er forget its tone,
Or the heart that spoke in glances
    Sympathetic with our own?

No, the flowers of spring may wither,
    While a fragrance still remains,
And a lute long, long forgotten
    Wake again its sweetest strains.

So the varied scenes that gather
    Often o'er life's changing way,
May obscure for days together
    All the glad things of that day;

But when memory turns the pages,
    Pausing only with the good,
Long she'll tarry with the warm hearts
    In that cabin near the wood.

WEDDING ANNIVERSARY.

The genial seasons come and go,
  Each in its time finds greeting,
From April's tearful overflow,
  Through summer's songs repeating,
When, sere, the autumn casts her leaves
  Where nature's heart is lying,
And o'er the year's well-gathered sheaves
  December's winds are sighing.

Each brings its weight of hidden woe,
  Each holds its joy supernal,
As through the drifts of winter's snow,
  Spring brings her blossoms vernal.
And clustering memories crown the years
  With more of joy than sorrow,
For love outlives grief's bitter tears,
  And wreathes with hope the morrow.

And blest the day that happy finds
  Surcease to loveless weeping,

And matehood's circlet links and binds,
    Love's tender sequence keeping ;
For sacred thrills that soulful lyre,
    When loving hands attune it,
Whose altar shrines the nuptial fire
    Which makes two souls a unit.

May many be these happy hours,
    Your nuptials in reviewal,
Strewn be your path with hope's fair flowers
    Each day bring joy's renewal ;
May time, that often wanton plays,
    Crown each year as your sweetest,
And make succeeding nuptial days
    Your happiest and completest.

And speed the years or swift or slow,
    Till life's romance is olden,
Though in your locks be threads of snow,
    May you have wedding golden.
And later still, when o'er life's bars
    Your feeble steps are treading,
May angel guests, beyond the stars,
    Give you celestial wedding.

SAN FRANCISCO, CAL., Jan., 1885.

FROM "SPIRITATHESIS."

THERE is no law of chance.
Though Nature's bosom pulses soft and slow,
Or with a heavier flood her rivers flow,
Sends her wild torrents fierce to rend a gorge,
Hurls her swift lightning from her vulcan forge,
Volcano's belching down her mountain steeps,
Or dark, coiled venom's pestilential sweeps,
Centers her furies in the human mind,
With passions carnal and to vice inclined,
With hunger like a vulture's in his eye,
Demoniac lust and fury raging high;
Or softer sheen on placid lake she draws
The silvery pencil of her gentler laws,
And pads of lilies white berim her lips,
Where crystal mirages the stars eclipse,
Gives to the winglet of the air a zest—
Reason or instinct, which?—to build its nest,
Wild beasts their cunning and their cowardice
To slay each other and shun man's device;

Or in her soft maternal moods she keeps
Her starry vigils, shining while she weeps,
Holding her children to her bosom pressed,
And gives them dreams of an eternal rest;
Divinest when to erring souls she nears
With mercy's tender and forgiving tears,—
Whatever is, is the effect of laws,
Obedient always to their parent cause.
When nature deviates, her range of chance
Lies in some unrestricted circumstance
Hidden within the matrix where she molds
The thing she gestates or to life unfolds.
Whate'er to harmony or discord tends,
True to some law her courses shape their ends.

R. P. Journal, Nov., 1872.

ACROSTIC.

Kate, I would that but by wishing,
    All that's fair might be your lot,
To some Magian would I whisper,
    Ever heed her lightest thought.

And should time in changing ever
    Note a shadow o'er her life,
Near her be thou, softly bending;
    Hear her in the hour of strife.

Oh ! watch o'er her, gentle Magian,
    Wake to joy her griefs or woes.
Ever with the golden sunlight,
    Strew the pathway where she goes.

Memphis, Tenn., Nov. 1863.

COMPENSATION.*

Life's retributive law is just :
    We harvest what is sown ;
The pangs we bring to others' breasts
    Must surely pierce our own.

Strong is the hand that builds the arch,
    Stronger the thought that plans ;
Swift is the lightning's flash of words,
    Fleeter the soul's commands.

Common the crucificial wood
    Stretched Calvary above,
Turned priceless sandal when baptized
    By more than human love.

* Impromptu, close of lecture, Metropolitan Temple, San Dec. 28, 1884.

COMPENSATION.

Clear is the eye that, o'er life's ills
    Transfixed, still lifts to heaven;
Greater the soul that here forgives
    The sin to be forgiven.

Bitter may be the blight of wrong
    That rankles the heart within;
But love, that waits, and time will prove
    The sinner above the sin.

Heaven is not won by easy steps,
    But over toilsome bars,
As over rugged mountain heights
    We climb to reach the stars.

But whatsoe'er the devious way,
    Be this the soul's sure screed,
That soul most helps its own advance
    That helps where others need.

And if to gain life's recompense,
    When heaven its records scan,
The angels make for him defense,
    Who lives or dies for man.

TO "BEESWAX."

REPLY TO LETTER FROM LA S——, WHO ISSUED THE IDEA IN PAMPHLET THAT HONEYCOMB WAS A FUNGUS GROWTH EVOLVED FROM EXCREMENT AND HEAT OF THE BODY OF THE BEE IN THE HIVE.

How are you, my "Beeswax," you horrible tease?
Your letter came duly, or your essay on Bees.
Though I'm sure I was struck with an "I dear" so funny,
That a foolish old bear should address me "My honey."

Your arguments many may sweetly discourse,
Yet to people of sense they will bear little force,
For philosophy that has to be "drawn" for a bee
Is too weak in its points for a woman to see.

For a man who advances an idea so dead
Must have some time been troubled with drones in his head,
That the busy and ever-industrious bee
Should wait while the comb-cells grow up like a tree.

TO "BEESWAX."

And you ask (why so foolish I'd never have guessed
If the comb into cells by the bee is compressed
And brought to the hive on its body in rings,
While you say you were too much afraid of their stings

To ever go close to their hives on a venture,
You are still on this topic an able commentor):
"Why in winter, when vegetation sleeps under the snow,
The comb in the hives should continue to grow?"

The numerous flakes that lie scattered about,
Seem all you desire to put that beyond doubt;
And did you but think that these flakes on the floor
Were the caps that have covered their sweet winter store.

But isn't it strange that these self-sealing cans
Should grow, to exclude all the air, without plans?
Since you're sticking to nature without an intent,
You must own I've an eye out for sweets that ferment.

Perhaps I am saucy to offer advice,
And your wrath may wax warm, if I do, in a trice,
But nevertheless my words would be these,
If you patiently watch you may still learn of bees.

And now I'll subscribe to this doggerel rhyme,
And serve you another dish some other time;
And as there could never be honey distilled,
Without Beeswax to spread out its caps to be filled,

You will pardon me now for addressing you so,
For "Honey" comes next after Beeswax, you know;
And I'll pledge you my word, still as friendly and true,
You'll find me the same, ever, Addie Ballou.

THE WORLD MUST HAVE ITS CRUCIFIED.*

FAR to the east, and many years ago,
    A village nestled near a wave-washed beach
Among the hills. A streamlet's silver flow
    Flecked o'er the landscape's distant reach.

High rose the swell of anthems on the air
    From steepled churches, on the sabbath day;
And high the flagstaffs, on the village square,
    Flung to the wind their freedom's pennons gay

On days of jubilee and on July the fourth;
    And on the streets no traffic of the week
Or roysterous voice of boys who sally forth,
    On sabbath days could any trespass make.

---

* This poem refers to an incident in the memory of childhood days that occurred in the native village of the writer (Chagrin Falls, Ohio), when that glorious woman, Abbie Kelly, afterwards Foster, came there to advocate the abolition of the Afro-American slave. The church bells were tolled as she departed on her self-appointed missionary work, whatever the little village may afterwards have done to redeem its unhappy part in this affair.

Meekly the parson read his weekly text:
    "As to the least of these, so do ye unto me,"
With comments. While the deacons, sitting next,
    With warm "Amens" responded, and resignedly

Turned down the edge of consciousness awhile,
    Nodding acceptance to the plea for grace,
And, with complaisance, at the close would smile
    And say, "Ours really is a very godly place."

And all the saintly women, in their pews,
    Smiled their approval o'er each restless fan—
"He is so good, our minister; I like his views—"
    And worshipped less the Maker than the man.

One day a stranger through the village gate
    Made entrance on a mission, all of love,
For an o'er-ladened race to supplicate,
    Each saintly heart in sympathy to move.

In modest mien and gentleness of heart,
    Yet with a fire of eloquence sublime,
Above the rabble in the public mart
    That voice was lifted in a cause divine.

But straight arose that godly little town,—
>Rose up indignantly with one accord,—
And said, while gathering the righteous frown,
>"This thing will never, never, please the Lord!

"In scripture rendering it would appear,
>However sore the need be of the human,
Saint Paul has made our duty clear,
>We must keep silence on the part of woman."

Then first in order (all the brethren led)
>The village scoffer who his time employs
With vicious rumor, or on scandal fed,
>And vulgar jests deals to the idle boys.

And so they gossiped round about the square,
>Prospecting on the moral of the case,
And felt abused that any woman dare
>To speak in public in their righteous place.

The perfect women drew their skirts aside,
>And sneered at very mention of her name,
And as she passed their way, indignant cried,
>"The wicked creature! Isn't it a shame?"

And so the whisper rose to be a din,
>   Until the very thunders seemed let down.
They said, "We cannot answer for this sin
>   Unless we send this woman from the town."

"They stoned the prophets in the olden time,
>   And Christ was buffeted in Galilee,
Joan of Arc they burned, and for no crime,"
>   She said : "What is there then for one like me?"

Then as the clustered village sank from sight,
>   To that lone figure, on her toilsome way,
The church bells clamored as at dead of night
>   The fire-cry calls the sleeper to the fray.

And still retreating from the noisy street,
>   The weary pilgrim from disgrace went out.
Toll! toll! ding! dong! the bell's funereal beat
>   Died on the air with mingled noise and shout.

To-day that silvered head is sweetly bowed
>   Beneath its coronet of peaceful age,
And justly is the nation fondly proud
>   To write her record on historic page.

SUISUN, CALIFORNIA, June 13, 1878.

GUILTY.*

Guilty! Yer Honor, I do not deny it;
I did what I could, sir, to help on the riot.
The right or the wrong of it I don't defend,
But where do these money sharps think it will end?

All the days of my life I was brought up to work,
And these hands of mine ain't no hands to shirk;
They be the willin'est hands, I'll be bound,
Nor stronger nor abler than them can be found.

I be a man for peace, too; but if the right
Can't come without it, then I'm for fight.
The mouths of the children, they must be fed,
For hunger, yer Honor, knows no law but bread.

Just look at me, Judge, do I look like a scamp,
Because bein' hungry has made me a tramp?
Do I look like a deadbeat, choosin' to roam,
If work could be had, and with comfort at home?

* *Daily Post.* Read by the author before the workingmen's mass meeting, San Francisco, August 26, 1877.

Cowardly, was it? Well, likely it may be;
But I never knowed fear, and I ain't no baby
To go whinin' about; nor I ain't no sneak
To pander and skulk when it's blows that must speak.

Why, I fit with Grant down the old Mississip,
And 'twas there where the cannon's red-hot iron lip
Spewed into my side such a foretaste of hell,
And tore off my leg with a fragment of shell.

I've stood picket duty with death like a ruffin,
Waist-deep in the swamps, without blanket or coffin,
To give decent rites to the dyin' when dead,
With a daily allowance—two slabs of hard bread.

And I ain't the old soldier to discount the war;
To help win or die was what I went for.
Nor they won't complain, the dead, there in their grav
Of the forfeit they made to make free men of slaves.

It was somethin', no doubt, to lie wastin' away
Dead-alive in the prisons, without letters or pay;
But I count it all in as a part of the cost,
And if victory ended it, nothin' was lost.

We took that for glory, but our Waterloo met
With a tax upon labor to pay the war debt;
With wages reduced to compete with cheap labor—
With Chinese for rivals and the freedman our neighbor.

Rights of property, sir! Why, all property gained
Is the right of the hand that by labor is stained,
Not the grasping monopolists', who selfishly hold
The result of the worker in fetters of gold,

While industry begs for a pittance for bread
That millions may pillow aristocracy's head.
Why, these very railroads, with sinews of steel,
Were blood-wrought from sinews that quiver and feel.

Shall they whose hands lifted the yoke off the slave,
Bend their heads to a yoke without effort to save
Their manhood, their honor, the cheek of the wife,
From the insults that crimson a beggarly life?

We are cursed by contractors, till labor no more
Means honest employment and homes for the poor.
If we're idle, we're paupers; if we work, we are slaves;
If we strike out for justice, we're branded as knaves.

And now, please, yer Honor, I plead to the charge;
I'm guilty of dealin' out justice at large.
But if ye'll allow me one question of grace,
Pray, what would yer Honor have done in my place?

AUTOGRAPH.

AN IMPROMPTU.

When Nature first in primal dress,
    With prentice hand adorning,
Flung over night her first caress,
    She named the glory Morning.

With vigor, strength, ambition, rife,
    No doubt of power betraying,
Morn represents the man in life,
    All else his will obeying.

But later, when the toilsome day
    Its fretful labor closes,
When weary heart and footsteps stray
    Where peaceful love reposes,

With tender touch of twilight spell,
    To soothe life's restive fever,
She named, like thee, her vespers well,
    Woman, Evangel, Eva.

Album, Miss Eva Conant.
    San Jose, California, Dec., 1883.

MY AMBITION.

Why should I stoop while others climb
    The starry steeps to fame?
Why should the fountains of success
    Forget to slake my flame?

Why should these arms forever grasp
    The vacant, empty air?
Why fly the hopes of my pursuit
    And vanish everywhere?

Why proudly stand on fortune's round
    Many whose deeds in life
Are not inwrought with more of good,
    Or half the wealth of strife?

My bleeding feet in vain pursue
    The paths that bloom for them,
And cheers are theirs from lips that part
    On me but to condemn.

MY AMBITION.

Not for the baubles of display
    Do I to fame aspire,
But that it crowns with brighter grace
    The strength of high desire.

Not for a badge of honor, bought
    At price of honor lost;
Not for position high in rank,
    That worth should be its cost;

Not for a gilded recompense,
    To pander to a pride;
Not that my bark adown life's stream
    Inanimate might glide;

But only that these unfledged powers,
    Lying conscious in my breast,
Might leap the confines of their tomb,
    And scale each mountain's crest.

That I might stand beside the brave
    Who dare defend the right,
And in the conflict, weak or strong,
    Be foremost in the fight.

That I might hurl to hungry ears
    The thunders of decree,
Anticipate, from things that are,
    The things that are to be.

Wake with authoritative mien
    The lethargy of men,
Tear down the altars of their wrongs,
    And build to right again.

Cleanse out the debris of their crimes
    By speech of tongue and pen,
Bring back the man from maudlin cups,
    Redeem the magdalen.

Give governmental power to men
    To till the idle fields,
That stretching o'er the trackless waste
    No sweet fruition yield.

Give industry to those who pace
    The pauper's listless beat,
And on the soil God gave man free,
    Each soul a home retreat.

MY AMBITION.

And that the purpose of a life
    Made strong by daily pain,
Be recognized by humane acts,
    As one not spent in vain.

And thus with all life's purpose spent
    In deeds that bless mankind,
Should memory's scroll enroll me still
    Round loving hearts entwined.

And when adown the silent stream,
    To bend life's yielding oar,
Be folded in love's angel arms,
    To wander never more.

Dec. 1869.

LINES IN A PORTFOLIO.*

Sweet remembrancer of friendship,
    On thy page a thought I'll trace.
Thanks, my friend, on memory's tablet
    Thine shall bear an honored place.

May you ever live in sunlight,
    And no lingering storm-cloud rest
O'er thy life ; enough of tempest
    Just to form a rainbow's crest.

May thy noon of life be glorious,
    Peaceful when thy day declines,
And no friend to thee less faithful
    Than the one who pens these lines.

* To "Esculapius," Overton Hospital, Memphis, Tenn., Feb. 10, 1863.

WHERE DO THE SEA-GULLS GO?

Away from the docks and the shipping
  That tangle the breast of the bay,
From the flutter of hands in the harbor,
  Our ship went sailing away.
And as the cannon's brazen lip
Boomed back farewell, from our good ship
    A score of snowy-breasted things
    Swooped low and drooped their downy wings,
    And rose and dropped with every swell,
    And cried in flutelike tones, "Farewell."

Up rose the winds, and the water
  In fury leaped forward and aft,
And the foam and the spume of the breakers
  Dashed over the decks of our craft,
Till rocked upon a gentler swell,
Our gallant ship uprose and fell.
    Still followed close those feathered things
    Who trip and swoop with noiseless wings,

Those restless birds, by day and night,
Who seaward wing their ceaseless flight.

Away and away o'er the ocean
    The track of our destinies lay,
Through the languor of tropical evening,
    Though the tropical languor of day,
While still a thousand leagues from shore
The watery waste we traverse o'er ;
    Like phantoms of an exile troop,
    Those pinions o'er the waters droop,
    And swing and curve, and dip the main,
    Then, rising, lift their plumes again.

And this I asked of the skipper :
    "Pray where do the sea-gulls go
When the ships which their white wings follow
    Go down with the wrecks below ? "
He smiled, and looking far away
Replied, " Ours do not go that way."
    Heaven grant him right ; and yet, and yet
    The hearts that break cannot forget
    Those who along the sea-gull's track
    Go out, but nevermore come back.

With a strange yet a sweet superstition,
    A nation as free as their wings
Believe that the bird of the ocean
    Good speed and prosperity brings.
The mariner o'er frozen seas
Thinks, too, the souls of men are these ;
    That angels of the so-called dead
    In these their own bright pinions spread,
    And, watchful of the wrecks and shoals,
    Bring safe to harbor human souls.

Whatever may be the tradition,
    A truth or a fancy of thought,
May the wing of our angel protect us,
    That calamity follow us not,
And lip to lip, and heart to heart,
May all yet meet who, wide apart,
    In different ways, by land or sea,
    Pursue life's varied destiny.
    Oh, white wings, bring at last our spars
    To harbor safe beyond the stars.

SHIPBOARD, ZEALANDIA, mid-ocean, June 19, 1885.
Bell, Auckland, N. Z.

WORMWOOD.

I said as I gazed on her ruined life,
   I could curse the wretch who had made it so;
And I set my teeth till my purple lips
   Were rigid and cold as my heart below.

I clutched my hand till the nails' keen edge
   Cut a furrow deep in my rigid palm;
I groaned aloud, "Has it come to this,
   That the wolf has ravished our sweet ewe lamb?"

Oh, God! what a thing is a woman's love,
   To be won at the cost of a life accursed,
To be flung like a worn-out sandal off,
   To slake the fever of passionate thirst.

TERRE HAUTE, IND., 1872.

MY DREAM OF SAINT VALENTINE.

I had a beautiful dream last night,
And bright was the vision that swelled on my sight
As the upper world, and as wondrous rare
As the zones that encircle the 'habitants there.

Sweet fancy lent me her golden wings,
And, swift as an unchained peri springs,
Far, far I sped through the ether blue,
Till the world in its darkness sank from view.

Then in sudden splendor I saw arise
The gates that open to Paradise.
Lo! the angel who waits in those arches wide
Is flinging the golden barriers aside.

I enter, it seems, with a noiseless tread;
I float in an air where fragrance is shed
As sweet as the astral zephyr's sigh
O'er the sea where the isles of the spices lie.

Now a gush of sweet harmony, liquid and clear,
Bursts forth like a charm on the ambient air;
Now it falls to a cadence, now rises and swells
Like the pealing tones of the chiming bells.

No bough ever waved under tropical skies,
But graces these gardens of Paradise;
No flower ever bloomed upon earth's fertile sod,
But blossoms more sweet in this valley of God.

No bird ever warbled in hawthorn or prune,
But sings in these bowers of eternity's June;
No hopeless wish of the human breast,
But finds in this heaven its want redressed.

I glanced where the notes of a musical strain
Came trembling up from a grass-green lane;
There a crystal fount in the sunlight played,
And hanging harps by a breath were swayed;

There countless groups o'er the wide expanse
Were circling round in a bridal dance.
No harem veil hides half the graces
That glow among their lovelit faces.

And I saw not amid that countless throng
One heart that beat for itself alone,
But each for another more fondly dear,
As if no sin were in loving here.

I sighed as I turned from the evergreen glade,
For I thought, these joys too soon will fade.
For I knew even then it was only a dream
That must die with the dawn like a boreal gleam.

As if answering back, a voice replied,—
'Twas he who waits in those arches wide,—
"Our joys renew with the changing years,
And it's always Saint Valentine's day in the spheres."

I woke; the vision forever was gone.
Like the hopes that spring fairest in youth's sunny dawn,
Or the dewdrop that rests on the lip of the flower,
It gladdens the heart though it live but an hour.

Chilton Republican, **Feb., 1861.**

NOT ALONE WITH THE NIGHT.

Not alone with the night,
For on billows of light,
Like the scintillant rays of the morning's glad sun,
Like a messenger dove,
Wings the spirit of love,
To crown and compensate each desolate one.

Love with love shall be blest,
Heart with heart shall find rest,
When life's turbulent billows shall lash them no more.
Though the waves and the tide.
Wide their moorings divide,
They will touch the same sands on the beautiful shore.

Not alone with the night,
Though the canker and blight
Like a vulture have fed on the quivering heart,
For the spirit of love,
Like the sweet mother dove,
Keeps watch o'er the nest till the young pinions start.

Lip to lip will be pressed,
Heart with heart will find rest,
When these hungering souls span their circlet of years.
Not alone with the night,
For an angel of light
Counts the beads of our worth by the falling of tears.

SONG STORY FOR THE LITTLE ONES.

AUNTIE.—So the little ones want me to tell them a story?
Well, what shall it be about?—"Old mother Morey?"
Or the poor little kitten that drowned in the well?
Or "Puss in Boots," and what befell
The "King of Carabas" and his brother?
Or "Little Jack," whose indulgent mother
Gave him a bean of such wonderful powers,
That it grew to the sky in a couple of hours,
And when it had grown to a wonderful tree,
He climbed to its top to see what he could see,
And there in its branches, as snug as a mouse,
A savage old giant had built him a house;
How he killed the old giant, and got all his money?

MARY.—No, we want to hear something that's jolly and
                funny.

JAMIE.—Oh, pshaw! can't you tell us a story that's new?
I know every one of those old stories through;
I'd like to hear one that is every bit true,

As long as my arm, and longer too.
Or you can make up one, I guess, that will do.

AUNTIE.—Well! let me see; will Johnnie be good,
And sit in his chair as a little man should?

KATIE.—I guess he had better be put in his bed,
For he'll go to sleep and nod off his head,
Then what shall we do for a Johnnie to tend?

JAMIE.—Put his dress on a pillow, a cap on the end;
   It won't make half the muss,
   And keep so much stiller,
   Nor get up such a fuss,
   Our pet, Johnnie's "piller."

KATIE.—Oh, go away, Jamie; don't pester him so;
You plague him so much he don't get time to grow.
There, Katie will take him right onto her lap,
And then if he likes he can take a nice nap.
And then his clothes, they will be such a pest,
Wouldn't the little boy first be undressed?
 There go his shoes, down onto the floor,
  Peep, little feet, I shall catch his toes,
   Out and in as they come and go,
   Under the folds of his robe of snow.
 See, just in this way, before he knows,

There, hush! Never mind, we won't tease any more;
There, cuddle his curly pate down on my breast.
      Lulla-by-by,
      Then shut up his eye,
And see how nice little Johnnie will rest.

  AUNTIE.—Well, now for the story. Well, children, get
      quiet,
And then if you'll listen well, auntie will try it.
Well, let me see; I must tell it in rhyme,
And begin the old way: "Once on a time,
There lived a man"——

  JAMIE.—That's just the way the story began
About that terribly wicked man,
Who strutted about in his beard of blue,
Who killed all his wives, and hung them, too.

  KATIE.—Are you telling the tale? You had better say
      less,
And listen while others are talking, I guess.

  AUNTIE.—Well, once on a time, a man and his wife
Who had never done any harm in their life,
Lived in a nice cottage just under the hill;
And the brook that rushed by turned the wheel of the
      mill,

Where the man worked on from day to day,
    Watching the grain from hopper to sieve,
  And for a lifetime spent in that way
    It was flowery enough for any to live.
For the cows and the pigs, and the colts and the sheep,
That would feed on the hillside or lazily sleep
Under the boughs of the spreading trees,
And that row of hives with their humming bees,
And the corn that grew in the further lot,
And the sunflowers tall that lined the walk
To the spring that welled from the old gray rock,
And the children that clambered upon his knee,
Boisterous with mirth and innocent glee,
Were his, all told; could he ask for more
To add its weight to his bountiful store?
Well, the miller worked on from day to day,
As free from care as his babes at play;
And the brook still flowed in its usual way;
And music sweet, like the miller's song,
Made cheery echoes the whole day long.
And everything seemed to be taking part
In the roundelay of his merry heart,
Just as everything wears a smile, you know,
When we are happy and see them so.

Amid the din of the dusty town,
    Lived in princely splendor a millionaire,
With his wife, a lady of this renown,
    For queenly beauty was none so fair.

But gold and glitter and queenly bride
    Were as empty bubbles that float on air,
For princes will starve if fed on pride,
    And so will the heart of a millionaire.

So, tired of the din of the crowded town,
    And loving the quiet of nature's ways,
And sick of the chill of his lady's frown,
    Viewed under the mask where beauty plays,

He wandered oft where the cooling shade
    Flung a darker green o'er vale and hill,
And often paused where the brook was stayed
    To turn the wheel of the gray old mill.

"Can you tell me why," said the millionaire,
    "Your life is ever so blithe and gay?
For your happy heart and rustic fare
    I would give my untold wealth to-day."

"Heyday!" said the man, with right good will,
    As he doffed his cap to the millionaire,
"My thanks are first to my busy mill,
    For it feeds the sources of all my care.

"It gives me labor, and that is wealth;
    These sinewy arms are mines of gold;
My cot is aglow with ruddy health,
    And virtue and love are never old.

"So all of the world was made for me,
    And I am akin to all that lives,
And whether I whistle to bird or tree,
    It always echoes what my heart gives."

The miller paused, but the millionaire
    A lesson had learned of priceless worth,
That the hidden springs of happiness are
    In the heart's pure fountain that gives them birth.

And now remember, my little pets,
    That life isn't always what it seems;
And never murmur with vain regrets,
    Though you fail to attain your golden dreams.

For happiness lies in the reach of all,
    And to give of goodness will make it ours;
And if the shadows and tempests fall,
    They but bring us the odor of broken flowers.

MANKATO, MINNESOTA, April, 1866.
R. P. Journal, Chicago.

THE BATTLE OF SHIPS ON MOBILE BAY, ON AUGUST 5, 1864.

Fair as a dream of Alhambra lay
Along the horizon a line of gray,
As morning crept softly o'er placid bay.

The air was balmy with sweet incense
Which ravished the shore with perfume intense,
For its torpor and heat a recompense.

Laden with odors from orange trees,
Came only a sigh of the lightest breeze,
To quiver the breast of the summer seas,

Like the smile that ushers prophetic gloom,
As calm that presages the dread simoom,
The song of the phœnix triumphant in doom.

While yet the morn's first pennons play,
The fleet already is under way
For the famous battle on Mobile Bay.

Girded together and two abreast,
Octorora and Brooklyn leading the rest,
Forward in line on the enemy pressed.

Boom! over the waters the first report,
The enemy's challenge comes from the fort;
And, boom! comes the enemy's quick retort.

Gun answers to gun in quick return,
Vomiting fire; from stem to stern
The ships seem in livid flame to burn.

Wildly the red-lipped cannons shriek,
Fixed is the bronzed old Admiral's cheek,
Command and courage his firm lips speak.

On, on, the marshalled mariners sped
Through the hot hail of fire and lead,
Tecumseh, with Cramer, this time ahead.

"*Hard a-starboard!*" commanded he,
And dashed straight on to the Tennessee;
Oh, God! what a sight was that to see!

Shaken as if by an earthquake shock,
Riven as if by a sunken rock,
A hidden torpedo midway she'd struck.

Headforemost plunging with all her brave ;
And Craven, while trying his pilot to save,
A hero went down in the pitiless wave.

Point Mobile, a living line of flame,
Red as the fires of Hades became,
But the command kept steadily on the same.

Shrapnel and canister, shell and grape,
Riddled with seam and many a gape ;
What from destruction could hope to escape ?

But what was the thunder of shot and shell ?
What were the fires of that threatening hell ?
His was to *do*, and to do it well.

And out of that day of smoke and flame
Rose many a hero's honored name,
And gave to the Admiral added fame.

For victory followed their deeds that day,
Who followed where Farragut led the way,
In that battle of ships on Mobile Bay.

SAN FRANCISCO, CAL., May 3, 1883.

AUTOGRAPH LINES.*

Since scores of friends indite the muse,
    In poesy to greet you,
Though mine can never fill their shoes,
    And limping goes to meet you;

Though others drink the choicest wine
    To you in pledges vernal,
Whose friendships are more close than mine,
    Though none the more eternal,

Accept at least one wish sincere,
    Though silent its expression,
Unless the angel of good cheer
    Inspire you by impression:

Believe at least, though prone to sin,—
    You know sin came through woman,—
No heart e'er beat a breast within
    More true to all that's human.

* Impromptu, Album, Wm. M. Ryder, San Francisco, Nov. 1881.

DEDICATION, WASHINGTON HALL.

BY LINCOLN POST, G. A. R.

Hail! comrades of the loyal host,
   Who wear the badge of honor,
Who, faithful to the nation's trust,
   When treason sat upon her,
Took up the armor of defense,
   Unswervingly to wear it,
To break the sword that gave offense,
   And tame the traitor spirit!
      So here's a toast
      To Lincoln Post,
We'll pledge it every one;
      Heaven prosper all,
      And bless the hall,
We name for Washington.

Here oft on memory's well-fought field,
   With riddled banners flying,
Will scattered foes retreat and yield
   Their captured dead and dying.

For time shall make these walls replete
   With many a thrilling story,
Which aging veterans repeat
   Of anguish and of glory.
      So here's a toast
      To Lincoln Post,
We'll pledge it every one;
      Heaven prosper all
      And bless the hall
We name for Washington.

Here pictured be the hallowed past,
   In memory's rehearsal,
As echoes on our dreams are cast,
   Successes or reversal.
Bivouacked on the tented plain,
   The camp fires smoldering glimmer,
With tramping armies through the rain,
   The lines of bayonets shimmer.
      So here's a toast
      To Lincoln Post,
We'll pledge it every one;
      Heaven prosper all,
      And bless the hall,
We name for Washington.

The picket and the skirmish line,
  That fluid in canteens, boys!
The forage, and the countersign,
  The mess of pork and beans, boys!
The contraband, the ambulance,
  The song and dance and juba,
The rebel matron's scornful glance,
  The "Glory hallelujah."
    So here's a toast
    To Lincoln Post,
We'll pledge it every one;
    Heaven prosper all,
    And bless the hall,
We name for Washington.

And sweetly still those oft-told tales
  Their text will be repeating;
Nor lost until remembrance fails
  To bring her welcome greeting.
Whate'er the chances to forget,
  Some note will still remind ye,
Some cherished chord make dearer yet
  "The girl I left behind me."

So here's a toast
To Lincoln Post,
We'll pledge it every one;
Heaven prosper all,
And bless the hall,
We name for Washington.

We'll pledge anew our cause to-night,
Renew the grip fraternal,
God and our country in the right!
Be loyalty eternal!
May charity, that star most fair
Of all the constellation,
Bless with her all-protecting care
The saviors of the nation.
So here's a toast
To Lincoln Post,
We'll pledge it every one;
Heaven prosper all,
And bless the hall,
We name for Washington.

THORNS INTERTWINE THE CROWN OF BAY.

O BLEEDING feet that steadfast climb
   The toilsome heights that rise afar !
O sleepless eyes whose light sublime
   Pales not the reflex of the star
Whose torch through night trails up the morn !
   O suppliant hands that clasp for aye !
O hearts with vigils racked and torn !
   Pierced is the brow that wears the Bay.

He may not reap the golden grain,
   Too late his sickle for the sheaf,
Nor feel the cooling plash of rain,
   Where burning sands invoke relief.
He may not pause where pleasures lure,
   Nor youth renew where children play,
But ever on with purpose sure
   Pursue, whose brow would wear the Bay.

He hears the cooling waters drip
    Down rocky basins, deep and cool,
Nor slakes the fever of his lip
    Beside the summer-verdured pool.
No moss-grown bank beguiles his rest,
    He may not note the nestling's lay,
Nor pause to clasp a maiden's breast,
    Thorns so entwine the crown of Bay.

He may not quaff the festive bowl,
    'Mid flowing wit and merry jest,
But he must heed the trumpet's call,
    And nerve his arm to greater zest,
Nor stay the tide on weltering field
    Of carnage red, where brothers slay,
To grave his name on glory's shield,
    And wear the blood-stained crown of Bay.

For him envenomed tongues distill
    Their viperous breath, to blight and curse,
With maledictions loud and shrill
    His noblest deeds would fain reverse;

But happy he, whate'er the cost,
    When stars light up his closing day,
Whose shield denotes no honor lost
    That he might wear the crown of Bay.

High as the overarching bars
    That gird the ever-widening skies,
Far-reaching as the eternal stars,
    O soul, for fame's imperial prize,
O'er rocks and deserts' boundless sands,
    Through haunted caves obscured of day,
Famished, unfed, on bounteous lands,
    Death brings at last the immortal Bay.

O'erwrought and toilful to the end,
    Sowing for other hands to reap;
Soul-hungering for a faithful friend,
    Unmourned, at last, to rest and sleep.
A century—and his resting-place
    Denotes his worth in tardy praise;
A benefactor to his race,
    A saint in marble, crowned with Bays.

Argus, SAN FRANCISCO, Christmas, 1891.

IN MEMORIAM.*

Farewell to thee, comrade ! Death's silence is over thee;
    Cold is the hand once so brave to defend
The emblem whose folds now so tenderly cover thee ;
    Peace to thee, patriot, comrade, and friend.
        All of life's history,
        All of death's mystery,
And all that the triumph of waking makes known,
Through rest, in promotion, at last is thine own.

Farewell to thee, comrade ! Where duty was known to thee,
    Faithful and true as the star to the pole ;
What was life's crucifix leave we alone to thee ;
    Only the angels may question the soul.
        Nature's supreme decree,—
        Death's final reveille,—
Summons thee higher and gives thee release ;
Be cherished thy memory; rest thou in peace.

* Suggested at the funeral of comrade Capt. C. P. Kelly, San Francisco, April, 1883.

Farewell to thee, comrade! Life's battle is o'er for thee;
  Death but endears what it cannot restore;
Surely eternity holds much in store for thee,
  Angels make welcome whom we most deplore.
    Close in with rank and file,
    We, too, must pass erewhile,
Then ripe for the summons that none can foretell.
Peace to thee, comrade! Till then fare thee well.

A MODERN PERI.*

ONE morn at the legislative gate
A woman stood disconsolate,
For well she knew, in her despair,
That none of her sex could enter there ;
Whate'er her grievance or great her wrong,
The lesser must yield to the will of the strong.
Awhile she listened to the din
Of arguments that clashed within,
Yet all with good intentions tending,
The people's honest cause befriending,
And caught a glimpse of the gold that flowed
From the people taxed, for their good bestowed.

"Alas !" she said, "it is awfully hard
From these rich endowments to be debarred."
"How happy," she thought, "these men must be,
In their cushioned chairs and abandon free,

---

* An impromptu with a meaning, during the legislature of 1880. *Sacramento Bee.*

Well fed and warmed." And yet she knew
They were weary with too much nothing to do.
"Why may not to me some sweet crumbs fall?
A common mother created us all."

The august Solons heard her pleading
For the orphaned lives that were interceding,
Then turned away with crocodile tear.
"Alas! no woman can enter here,
At least—unless—well, hardly any.
You see, my dear, they number so many.
But stay," he cried, "one chance might be;
Put in your claim for a clerk," said he.
"Child of a frail, angelic sex,
To aid your cause we would break our necks."

Then a partisan imp flew down from the wall,
And in passing gave an unearthly squall.
"They are giving you taffy—he! he! ha! ha!
I wish you success. Farewell, ta-ta!"

"I'll go," she said, "to the richest caves
In the sea of memory's murmuring waves.
There's a pearl wrought out of a grateful tear,
Down, down in the past of a scarlet year."

So lifting the wing of a speeding thought,
She trembling stood by the hallowed spot.
On a smoking field, with carnage red,
One face she lifted, her loved and dead.
"See, this I gave, but rest thou alone."
Away she sped to a dying moan.
And a smile lit up the parching lips
As they quaffed the cool drink, and her finger-tips
Strayed gently over his fevered head,
Then on to the next, and to each she said,
"God bless you, boys, and the mothers of men
Who made you so noble." They answered, "Amen."
"See, see!" she cried, as she stood at the gate
Whose hinges turn on the pivot of state—
"See, here is blood on a lock of hair,
And the grateful wish of a loved one's prayer,
Soldiers restored to the thinning ranks."
"For this the country returns you thanks.
Be thus contented, for that, you know,"
Said the senator soldier; "was long ago.
Some other tactics you'll have to try,
Though the 'open sesame' be very nigh;
Constituents first, and men that live,
Claim all the positions the state can give.

Try something stronger than this, my dear;
We're bound you yet shall have something here."
And one of them said with a knowing wink,
"We'll tire these women out soon, I think."
And drawing a sigh from his manly breast,
"Oh, shortly these women will give us a rest!"
Yet she knew as she scanned the beardless faces
Around the committees, for clerkship places,
That they would be voters by and by.
And yet again she said, "I'll try;"
Though she knew, whatever the promised truce,
Masculinity cooketh the woman's goose.

Then again the voice with unearthly yell,
"Are they giving you taffy again? Well, well."

With hopes all a-droop, like a wet mother hen
She clucked to her brood, but, alas! there and then
She learned what it was to be patient and wait,
And the justice that comes through the servants of state.

Where there's no inclination there's always excuse,
And a hopeful refusal is less than abuse.
But, oh! to be told—we are all of us human—
"If you want to be favored, why, don't be a woman;

At least don't grow old.   Leave us with the laws.
We'll care for your children if they should give cause;
That's why we have prisons and courts and all that,
And the poor-house for you, when you're old, sick, and flat."

"For favors? Why, even there's value in blood,
And color is foremost, as is well understood.
Go, woman! content to look over the wall,
The ballot alone ope's the doorway to all."

Once more the vulture, with mocking shriek,
Dropped venom from his gall-tipped beak:
"Why don't you do as the millions do—
Give back the taffy they give to you?"

MEMORIAL POEM.*

No. 1.

Scatter the garlands of roses,
    And all the sweet blossoms of May,
Above each low mound that encloses
    The perishing patriot's clay.
They who went out in the glory
    Of hope and the rapture of life,
To fields that were smoking and gory,
    And were foremost to lead in the strife,
Oh, cover them tenderly ; over them all,
Like a mantle of love, let the sweet blossoms fall.

They were the truest of brothers,
    They were the bravest of men ;
And the pride of the Roman mothers
    Was blessed in our sons again.
For what was the smoke of battle
    Or the thrust of sabre or sword,

---

* Read by Miss O'Brien, the elocutionist, Memorial Day and also evening, May 31, 1880, Sacramento, Cal.

The cannon's or musketry's rattle,
    To national honor restored?
Then cover them tenderly; over them all,
Like a mantle of love, let the sweet blossoms fall.

Guarding the dangerous passes,
    With never a heart dismayed,
Down by the poison morasses,
    Where pestilence indolent stayed,
Down by the turbulent river,
    And marching on to the sea,
Yet guarding the colors forever,
    Whatever the danger might be.
Then cover them tenderly; over them all,
Like a mantle of love, let the sweet blossoms fall.

See what they gave us in dying!
    O banner undimmed of your stars,
The grasses above where they're lying,
    Oh, kiss with the sweep of your bars,
For never again will they wake them,
    Or recall them to duty or pain.
Let our gratitude never forsake them,
    Who sleep 'neath the dew and the rain.

But cover them tenderly; over them all,
Like a mantle of love, let the sweet blossoms fall.

   Over the clustering tresses
     On brows that were white as the snow,
   On lips that some memory kisses,
     So speechless and silent below,
   Hands we have clasped so tightly,
     Arms so protecting and brave,
   Prized we not all too lightly,
     Till hid by the pitiless grave?
Then cover them tenderly; over them all,
Like a mantle of love, let the sweet blossoms fall.

   In the star-fretted evening, often,
     When the night with her gems is set,
   Sad mem'ries our hearts will soften,
     Of comrades we cannot forget;
   And we'll weep for the manly graces,
     Lying under the silent clay,
   And weep for the tear-stained faces,
     They left when they went away.
Then cover them tenderly; over them all,
Like a mantle of love, let the sweet blossoms fall.

And millions of duskier faces,
   Forever above their graves,
Will bless these, while history traces
   They died to make men of slaves.
Then let us rejoice, for the angel
   Who laurels the deeds of worth
Hath sent us a nation's evangel,
   And peace is again upon earth.
Then cover them tenderly; over them all,
Like a mantle of love, let the sweet blossoms fall.

For the grandest of nations no longer
   With the spirit of anger is rife;
And each year shall be riveted stronger,
   The hearts that were foes in the strife.
And at last when the final muster
   Calls each to the ramparts above,
Around him his comrades will cluster,
   With charity, friendship, and love.
Then cover them tenderly; over them all,
Like a mantle of love, let the sweet blossoms fall.

MEMORIAL POEM.

No. 2.*

SCATTER above them the garlands of blossoms,
   And laurel them all, these dead heroes of ours.
So still are the hands that are crossed on the bosoms
   Of those who lie sleeping beneath the bright flowers.
How brave were their hearts when in peril the nation
   Was tossed on the waves of dissension and death,
And war's crimson hand scattered wild desolation,
   Bringing terror and woe on the South's sultry breath.
     Then tenderly down on the grass and the clover
     Scatter the blossoms and cover them over,
     Father, and brother, and husband, and lover.

* Written for and read Memorial Day services, Opera House, San Francisco, Cal., May 31, 1880.

Cover the forms we had hopefully cherished,
  Hands we have clasped in love's tender embrace;
Oh! we grieve that our darlings so early have perished
  In the pride of their manhood, their beauty, and grace.
Oh, the beautiful curls and the soft sunny tresses,
  Mouldering and damp with the blight of decay!
Lips cold and still some sweet memory presses,
  Again their sweet smiles o'er the ruby curves play.
    Then tenderly down on the grass and the clover
    Scatter the blossoms and cover them over,
    Father, and brother, and husband, and lover.

Beautiful eyes we so loved are forever
  Shut out from the light and the glory of day,
And we weep as they wept at the parting, for never
  Will the shadow and blight on our hearts pass away.
Oh, long were the years to lie silent and lonely,
  If death were the sequel to duty and pain.
And for us they have died, for such recompense only
  As falls to the heroes who die not in vain.
    Then tenderly down on the grass and the clover
    Scatter the blossoms and cover them over,
    Father, and brother, and husband, and lover.

Blanched were the cheeks of the mothers who bore them,
  When the clarion of duty called their sons to the fray,
But never their prayers to their breasts can restore them,
  Who thus in their manhood were summoned away.
Like the mothers of Sparta, their anguish defying,
  They laid the bright sword on the national shield,
And bade them be brave, though the leaden hail flying
  In death-dealing terror swept over the field.
    Then tenderly down on the grass and the clover
    Scatter the blossoms and cover them over,
    Father, and brother, and husband, and lover.

May forever unsullied the banner float o'er them,
  Who shed their red blood for the red of its bars;
Oh, proud be the folds that in battle upbore them,
  To save from dishonor, who died for its stars,
And long may the nation her flowers above them,
  Begem with her laurels each patriot's grave,
And gratefully prove that we honor and love them,
  Whose lives paid the forfeit a million to save.
    Then tenderly down on the grass and the clover
    Scatter the blossoms and cover them over,
    Father, and brother, and husband, and lover.

And for those sadly lost with the nameless and missing,
   Where no hand can scatter love's tribute to-day,
A monument build in your hearts filled with blessing,
   And forget-me-nots twine in the chaplet of bay.
For white are their deeds who, as shoulder to shoulder,
   Go down in the fury of merciless wars ;
And white was the angel who summoned the soldier
   Whose muster records him among the bright stars.
     Then tenderly down on the grass and the clover
     Scatter the blossoms and cover them over,
     Father, and brother, and husband, and lover.

But the Bethlehem star of our nation has risen,
   And peace spreads again the white fleece of her wing;
No more o'er the plains shall the batteries glisten,
   And the war cry, "To arms!" down the broken lines ring.
And they who were bravest where duty was calling,
   Are first after peace to be brothers again.
And proud over all is our flag softly falling,
   Where freedom and peace o'er a happy land reign.
     Then tenderly down on the grass and the clover
     Scatter the blossoms and cover them over,
     Father, and brother, and husband, and lover.

And we know when at last over life's fretful ocean,
   The shadow of night o'er each veteran falls,
And the angel above gives to valor promotion,
   And to Death's final muster the patriot calls,
That marshalled a-near in the ether to greet them,
   With "Abraham" leading the armies above,
Their glorified comrades will cluster to meet them
   With charity, friendship, and brotherly love.
     Then tenderly down on the grass and the clover
     Scatter the blossoms and cover them over,
     Father and brother, and husband, and lover.

MEMORIAL POEM.

No. 3.

A<small>H</small>! we sadly remember that star-fretted morning,
  When only a cloud swept athwart the pale east,
Yet e'er midday was muttered a nation's wild warning,
  And at sunset with gloom all our sky overcast.
For flash upon flash, and with voice of the thunder,
  A challenge from Sumter, with death on the air,
Gave never a moment to pause or to wonder,
    The three hundred thousand equipped for the war.
      Droop softly and low o'er the mounds below,
      Flag of our country and lilies of snow;
      Kiss the green grasses that over them grow.

Brave were the hearts of the wives and the mothers,
  Who gave up their dearest, their husbands and sons;
Ah! they were the truest, the grandest of brothers
  That e'er faced an enemy's threatening guns.

They were the pride of our homes and the nation,
  Stalwart of heart as their patriot sires
Who defended the right against foreign dictation,
  When the old "Revolution" had kindled her fires.
    Droop softly and low o'er the mounds below,
    Flag of our country and lilies of snow;
    Kiss the green grasses that over them grow.

Oh, the long weary months of suspense and of waiting,
  Of praying, of fearing, of absence and tears;
Through the vigils of night, with a faith unabating,
  Till the anguish of months made the compass of years.
And many with hopeful good-by at the parting
  Came nevermore back to our bosoms again.
Where they fell on the field are the wild grasses starting;
  Where they sleep fall the dews and the summer-time rain.
    Droop softly and low o'er the mounds below,
    Flag of our country and lilies of snow;
    Kiss the green grasses that over them grow.

O beautiful eyes on whose lids are forever
  The kiss and the tears and the mildew of death,

From your home with the stars do you watch for us
    never ?
Do your lips never speak in some sweet blossom's
    breath ?
Oh, they sleep yet they rest not, for over and over
    They walk by our side in the land of our dreams,
And softly as falleth the dew on the clover
    Or the shimmer of stars on the bosom of streams.
        Droop softly and low o'er the mounds below,
        Flag of our country and lilies of snow ;
        Kiss the green grasses that over them grow.

And sometimes the touch of these perishing fingers,
    Now pulseless and cold on the bosoms below,
Seems clasped with our own, while fond memory lingers
    Like the perfume of violets under the snow.
And sometime we know that our eyes shall behold them
    When the summers and winters are over and gone,
In the land of hereafter our arms shall enfold them,
    Where death never takes from our bosoms our own.
        Droop softly and low o'er the mounds below,
        Flag of our country and lilies of snow ;
        Kiss the green grasses that over them grow.

MEMORIAL POEM.

Year after year how the comrades are passing
   The river of mists to the shadowy land,
And white are the feet that while evermore crossing
   Leave naught but their print on the desolate sand,
Till all shall be gone but a legend, a story,
   The sword of the grandsire, a rusted carbine,
A uniform covered with dust and with glory,
   In the garret a knapsack and soldier's canteen.
      Droop softly and low o'er the mounds below,
      Flag of our country and lilies of snow;
      Kiss the green grasses that over them grow.

And white are the plains where bivouac the angels
   Whom Death on his roll-call has mustered on high,
Where picketed still are the nation's evangels,
   The vanguard that guides on our march to the sky.
And at last when each veteran's name for promotion
   Is called to advance with the last countersign,
The angel on guard, for heroic devotion,
   Will bid him "fall in" with the heavenly line.
      Droop softly and low o'er the mounds below,
      Flag of our country and lilies of snow;
      Kiss the green grasses that over them grow.

So let the children of soldiers spread o'er them
  A mantle of blooms, and bedew with their tears
The graves of the heroes who, in valor before them,
  Gave to country their lives to win freedom for theirs.
Then gratefully let us remember and cover
  With flowers and the folds of our banner's bright bars
The graves of the sire and the son and the lover,
  Who died for mankind and the union of stars.

    Droop softly and low o'er the mounds below,
    Flag of our country and lilies of snow ;
    Kiss the green grasses that over them grow.

SACRAMENTO, CAL., May 31, 1881.

CHANCELLORSVILLE.

(KEENAN'S THREE HUNDRED.*)

In the deepening gloom of the forest of pine,
Three hundred horsemen were stirrupped in line.
Here were the batteries, broken and routed ;
Dismayed, panic-stricken, the wild rabble shouted.

* It was one of those tragic episodes of the war at Chancellorsville when sunset found our army badly confused and disorganized and driven wildly along its center. General Sickles' battery and General Pleasanton's cavalry were nearly a mile away and were not in order, but were "parked" awaiting orders. And General Howard's Eleventh Corps were completely surprised. On came Stonewall Jackson's immense corps, pursuing the fugitives of infantry, artillery, ambulance, pack mules, negroes, and stragglers. Nearer and nearer through the woods came the Confederates' yell and the rush of Jackson's victorious legions, twenty thousand strong. General Pleasanton, riding in front of the guns, saw that delay was the only way to prevent our utter demolition, and he gave to Major Keenan, who rode at the head of three hundred horsemen, the order so fatal to him, yet which alone saved the day. Said he, "Major, you must charge into those woods with your men and hold the enemy in check till I get these guns in position. You must do it at all costs." Keenan replied, "It's the same as saying you must be killed," but with a smile he added, "General, I'll do it." They made the charge, delayed Stonewall Jackson's famous corps until Sickles' came up with reinforcements, and the day was saved.

Artillery, infantry, maddened by fright,
Confused and disordered, took refuge in flight.
Commands out of order were given at random,
Ambulance, pack-mule, and stragglers in tandem,
'Mid thunders of cannon and shrieking of shell,
The fugitives flying, the Confederates' yell,
The smoke and the carnage, the impress of hell,
 They rode as never men rode before,
 Rider and horse, to return no more!
 They bravely rode and they bravely fell,
 At the close of that day at Chancellorsville

Flashed and shimmered the grand display,
The gleam of sabre and bayonet's play,
Along the sunset a line of gray,
Of the legion, less than a mile away.
Twenty thousand followed the lead
Of Stonewall Jackson's silvered head,
As hurrying fast and hurrying faster,
To make more sure our dire disaster,
Pressing closely upon us then,
Like a wall of death, came Stonewall's men.
 To meet them, as never men rode before,
 Rider and horse, to return no more;

Undaunted they rode who so nobly fell
At the close of that day at Chancellorsville.

Then suddenly forward, in front of the guns,
Rode stern, brave General Pleasanton.
"Align those pieces," commanded he.
Oh for time to impede that human sea
E'er it sweeps us down!—but an hour's delay
To rally in order! It would save the day.
Delay we must the advancing host,
Engage their column or all is lost.
Too late to reckon the terrible cost,
They rode as never men rode before,
Rider and horse, to return no more;
They rode to death, but they glorious fell
At the close of that day at Chancellorsville.

Three hundred brave horsemen Keenan led.
"Charge into those woods," the General said.
"Whatever the cost to your noble head,
Keep them in check till we right our guns."
Through his veins the blood of a hero runs.
One moment, a flash of his eagle eye,
Then his brow reflected the sunset sky

As he bared it, responsive to the command.
Then with a sweep of his manly hand,
"I'll do it, General! It is only to die!
But where duty calls loudest there ever am I."
  They rode as never men rode before,
  Rider and horse to return no more,
  Keenan's three hundred, who grandly fell
  At the close of that day at Chancellorsville.

All honor to those who, thus quick to obey,
To their death hurried forward and saved us the day.
Glory has known other heroes before,
But bravery was never deserving of more.
They died, yet they live in the nation's warm heart;
On the tablets she notes they have graven their part,
And the star that most radiant evermore keeps
Bright vigil above where a patriot sleeps.
And remembrance each season fresh chaplets will bind,
Till our feet, marching on to that city, shall find
The heroes who bravely have died for mankind.

With those who rode as never before,
From earth to eternity's beautiful shore,
The immortal three hundred who gallantly fell
At the close of that day at Chancellorsville.

SAN FRANCISCO, CAL., Feb. 15, 1883.

THE CHARGE UPON THE HILL.

Nightfall darkened down the mountain, stifled seemed
    the silent air,
Heavy with portending omens that preceded strife of
    war.
Moonbeams pencilled through the hollys, shadowed o'er
    the river's breast,
As the troops upon the hillside stacked their arms and
    went to rest.

Midnight's hour, and all was silent as the garden of the
    dead,
Save the watchword of the sentries pacing on with meas-
    ured tread,
And the rushing of the river. Slowly up the smoke-cloud
    crept
From the many smoldering camp-fires; all was silent,
    nature slept.

Morning came; dread consternation spread throughout
    the circling camp,
And the distant hills reëchoed with the horseman's heavy
    tramp.

And the clanging and the shouting of the fast approaching foe
Thrilled the hearts that beat for freedom, with a patriotic glow.

On they came, that charge of horsemen; fearful raged the deadly strife,
Till the river's current, ebbing, seemed a tide of human life.
Now they waver! now they rally! foot to foot and hand to hand;
Now they strike those rebel colors! now they falter!— see, they run!

Victory! Ah! we have conquered; heroes, ere you sink in death,
See the starry emblem triumph, bless it with your dying breath!
See the shattered host retreating, how they scatter as they run!
God is with us! we have beat them, and the field is fairly won.

Heaps of mangled forms, and dying, lay upon the trampled sod;
Heaps of breathless forms were lying, they were gathered home to God.
Filling up the gaping trenches with the foemen's fallen dead,
Where the panic-stricken scattered, where they left them when they fled.

One among the fallen heroes crept beneath a shadowy bough,
And the death-dew slowly gathered o'er his pale and manly brow,
And his dying eyes grew brighter with a new and sudden light,
As the memory of the homestead crowded in with visions bright.

And his husky voice grew fainter, sank to whispers weak and low:
"Comrade, raise me—I am going—feel my pulses, how they go;

Wet my lips—then listen to me—for my strength is failing
    fast;
Lay your palm upon my forehead till this fearful pain is
    past.

"You will go and see them, won't you?"—then his eyes
    grew dim with tears—
"Tell my mother I would gladly comfort all her failing
    years.
But the Father who has called me careth for a lonely
    heart;
We shall meet in the hereafter where the loving never
    part.

"Many others on the altar of our country's cause have
    laid
Lives as precious to another as the sacrifice she made.
To my gray-haired patriot grandsire, only this to him I'll
    say,
Through the hottest of the battle I have bravely fought
    to-day.

"Tell my sister—give me water—tell her never to regret
That she gave her soldier brother—tell her I did not
    forget

All the counsels that she gave me—oh, she tried to be so brave,
As she said, 'I fear, my brother, you will fill a soldier's grave.'

"There's another, not a sister—closer bend your face to mine—
It is Katie!—yes? you know her—oh, I know her heart will pine
For the words of tender meaning—she was fragile as a flower—
Tell her that I kept her image foremost, even in the battle hour.

"Raise me quick! I'm sinking—fainting—and I long once more to gaze
Where the dear old starry banner o'er the field triumphant sways.
Farewell, comrade!" Then a quiver shook his frame, and all was still.
And they laid him with the heroes of the charge upon the hill.

LONG AGO.

There's a stream whose crystal waters
    Lave the sands of golden hue;
There's a cottage twined with roses,
    Spangled o'er with morning dew;
There the summer-scented clover
    And the violets used to grow,
When the feet of guileless childhood
    Pressed the banks of long ago.
        Long ago! how memory lingers!
        Touched again by angel fingers
Are the chords that sweetly murmur
    Of the golden long ago, long ago.

Eyes that beamed with loving meaning,
    Hands that smoothed our couch of rest,
Closed to look no more upon us,
    Folded on a pulseless breast.

Like the drifting flecks of shadow
    Where the water-lilies grow,
So the threads of silken tresses
    Floated from us long ago.
        Long ago! how memory lingers!
        Touched again by angel fingers
Are the chords that sweetly murmur
    Of the golden long ago, long ago.

We shall cross that mystic river,
    When love's partings come no more;
We shall clasp the waiting angels
    Of the loved and gone before,
By and by, some glad to-morrow,
    When life's tide shall outward flow,
When the shadows now about us
    Shall be with the long ago.
        Long ago! how memory lingers!
        Touched again by angel fingers
Are the chords that sweetly murmur
    Of the golden long ago, long ago.

SPRINGFIELD, OHIO, 1871.

RECEPTION TO PAUL VANDERVOORT, GRAND COMMANDER, G. A. R.

Thrice welcome to our Golden Gate,
    Our comrade and commander,
Proudly the tribute of our state,
    In welcome, we surrender.

Much claims he from the soldiers' hearts;
    Worth makes the comrade dearer;
Who honor to our cause imparts
    Is still our color-bearer.

The soldier then is comrade still,
    Around him fondly cluster
Such greetings of our right good will,
    To this our general muster.

The serried years of time's recruit,
    Since camping out together,
Have put the enemy to rout;
    We now are one forever;

Have furrowed lines on many a brow,
    And many locks have whitened ;
Age many a form has made to bow,
    And death our ranks has lightened.

Still memory holds a full canteen,
    Though comrades are divided
As wide as oceans are between ;
    Our kinship is decided.

Remembrance sees the curling smoke
    Where lingering camp fires smolder,
Repeats the song and merry joke ;
    The hymn book of the soldier

Brings from its well-planned hiding-place
    (Would you suspect?) a hard tack,
With all a soldier's sinful grace,
    His euchre deck—a card pack !

We've marched together, hot and cold,
    We've messed, yes, drank, together,
Though oft the fiction has been told,
    'Twas only when the weather—

Too much swamp land had filtered through,
  Or dried up all the water.
Was any soldier known to do
  Or drink what he'd not " oughter "?

And forage? No, we never did;
  Believe it not, O stranger,
Unless some straying chick or kid
  Came in the way of danger.

The war is past, but yet the roll
  To duty still is calling,
Each day some overladened soul
  Death's scout is overhauling.

Each on his beat must picket wait,
  Life's field knows no retreating,
Till, challenged at the outer gate,
  His countersign repeating,

He lays life's knapsack down at last,
  Life's charges all exhausted.
Be this the tribute o'er him cast :
  " His scabbard never rusted."

One toast then, comrades, to our guest,
Be never welcome grander :
Be everywhere his mission blest,
God speed our Grand Commander.

May 5, 1883.

AUTOGRAPH LINES.

IMPROMPTU, TO MARY ———.

From the cares that hedge thickly life's troublesome way,
    May your pathway forever be free,
And cloudless your sky as o'er midsummer's day,
    As your life bark sails over its sea.

And when the gray twilight of evening appears,
    May its coronet star to the night
Bring happy reflections of good through the years,
    And guide you still on by its light.

May blessings more rare than the treasures of earth
    To the hopes of the toiler impart,
The wealth that compensates the soul for its worth
    Be yours for your goodness of heart.

Fond du Lac, Wis., Oct., 1881.

SAINT MARGARET.*

From that bright zone which belts the space
Where dwell the angels of our race,
The glory of whose shining bars
Exceeds the radiant light of stars,
There came one day, with noiseless tread,
One who had joined the so-called dead.
And o'er each well accustomed place,
The yearning spirit's eager trace
   Swept light o'er all, and strong and tender,
   He clasped a maiden fair and slender;
Fairest of fair was her sweet young face.

---

* To Mrs. E. B. Crocker ("Aunt Margaret"), who built a conservatory for flowers at the cemetery in Sacramento, that the poor might have flowers free to scatter above the dead. Written for reading at a floral festival tendered to her by the city of Sacramento, May 6, 1885.

And o'er the lily bloom of health
And tint of lips, there came by stealth
The pallor o'er the flush of pain,
Till as the snow untouched of stain,
Transfixed among that saintly host,
She who by all was loved the most
Ere she became an earthly bride,
Became the bride of death, and died.
   And who shall say but that spirit lonely
   Had need of the comfort of this flower only,
To twine his own with her love's rich wealth?

And far away that tearful train
Crossed mountain and wide stretch of plain,
That she, asleep, at last might lay
In that loved home for one brief day,
And then forever find repose
Where Sacramento murmuring flows,
And flowers perpetual bloom above
The casket hallowed by such love.
   Thus loving and tender they bore the maiden,
   With hearts and with lids with tears o'erladen,
Fairest of fair, to her home again,

Among her birds and books and flowers,
Where passed her childhood's happy hours,
Where pictured, heavy hung the walls,
In boudoir and in spacious halls,
And all who knew her tribute paid.
The poor who loved the gentle maid
Bowed low their heads and breathed a prayer
Of benediction o'er her there,
  Beautiful still and so sweetly sleeping,
  One angel more her love-watch keeping,
Radiant and pure in the heavenly bowers.

Each day the mother's loving care
Bestrewed the grave with blossoms rare,
And as they fell with fragrant cheer,
Her angel seemed to draw more near.
And near the flower-strewn mound one day,
An humble cortège wound its way.
One meager tribute there was laid
Upon the mound but newly made.
  A kindred sorrow makes one human.
  The heart of this noble, loving woman
Was moved in their sweet, sad grief to share.

She saw them bowed with grief's regret.
"What boon can make despair forget?"
She asked. "To this bright home of ours,
For these a transport build of flowers,"
Whispered a voice she loved so well.
A pure white lily downward fell,
And lay a-tremble at her feet,
And tinged the air with odors sweet.
   The poor pray heaven, "All good defend her,
   May always the angels of light attend her."
The angels call her Saint Margaret.

SAN FRANCISCO, May, 1885.

AUTOGRAPH.

ALBUM, MASTER LEE STEELE.

Some think, to be happy and blithe and gay,
   And to never know care or sorrow,
You never should try to do to-day
   What you can put off till to-morrow.

But for happy-go-lucky (but, pray, don't tell)
   I would rather do nothing at all ;
Still if one must do, why, to do that well
   And at once pays the best for us all.

But the surest way out of life's troubles and pains,
   If to-morrow we wish to be jolly,
And if in the end we would treasure some gains,
   Is to-day to keep clear of its folly.

MERCED, CAL., March, 1885.

THE OLD AND THE NEW.

As dark as the shore-hidden lake of Avernus,
  When storm-crouching clouds run the billows before,
While a spectre leads onward wherever we turn us,
    Where, forever recoiling, the voice of the thunder
    Makes moan till the caverns seem riven asunder,
    Recur to my thought the strange visions of old,
    And the rhythm of the story the sages have told
Wails out like a sob on the night evermore.

And backward we glance through the shadows that thicken
  With the smoke and the flame and the hurrying horde;
Where the carnage appalls on our souls till they sicken,
    And pillage leads onward its spoils to the slaughter,
    And breast of the babe and the virginal daughter
    Are bared to debauch; and the bosoms of snow
    Lie trampled and torn, and the ebb and the flow
Of the tide of the years in the tumult are heard.

And the winds from afar bring the sickening savor
  From battlefields damp with the mould of the slain,
Who fell in despair o'er a hopeless endeavor,
    Who died for a creed or a sacred tradition.
    And the rivers run red where a strange superstition
    Appeases its god with the dimple and smile
    Of the prattler. While yonder the funeral pile
Dyes crimson the sky o'er the orient plain.

And red are the jaws of the tigers that, restless,
  Gnash sharp on the bars that confine in their prison;
And the whelps they have suckled are fattened and zestless,
    And sniff the keen scent of the victims advancing.
    The headsman's keen sword from its scabbard is glancing,
    And the shield of a Pilate is shimmering bright,
    And a halo of stars breaks the seal of the night,
Where a crucified Christ is o'er Calvary risen.

And down through the ages, when prophet or priestess
  Has lifted the veil from the terrible night,
Consigned to their doom-haunted prisons, releaseless,

Have died by the hemlock, the stake, and the gib-
bet;
And the scourge of the bigot has rendered its
tribute,
Till heaven looking down through its numberless
stars,
Receding appears, and its crystalline bars
Seem draped with the weeds of despair and of blight.

An empire of woe, and a doom of despairing,
With Death, the grim despot, crowned monarch
alone.
To destroy and destroy, with no hopeful repairing,
For the hope-slayer builds never transport from
sorrow,
Illumines no tomb with a happier morrow,
But in living, to perish, in death after death,
With the rolling and seething and sulphurous
breath
Of Inferno, while Pluto exults on his throne.

With weeping is fretted the heart of the human,
The tears that undo not the fetters of wrong.
What profit the anguish and travail of woman,

When the sons she has borne and her bosom has
    nurtured
Are sold like the beast, and are driven and tor-
    tured,
Pursued through the cypress, and mourn and en-
    treat
To the night, while close at the fugitives' feet
The bay of the bloodhound sounds dismal and long?

Thus backward in shadow my sad soul, reviewing,
  Wove dark in the background the woof of the old,
With naught but the sorrowful measure construing,
    And all discontent that my thought could en-
        gender;
    And naught in the present seemed blissful and
        tender.
    Then the plume of a sceptre my vision o'er-
        drew;
    An angel rebuked me, "See, here is the new!"
And traced on the meshes in letters of gold.

And where perished the prestige of leader or nation,
  There uprose, like a phœnix, illumined and white,
Transfigured in death, into life's consummation.

And they who have patiently suffered their losses,
Have dared to be right, still enduring their crosses ;
And they who for love of their fellows have died,
Who with right on their shields have all error defied,
As the stars, shine forever as guides of the night.

Till upborne and upborne on the purple of morning,
With shafts of gray splendor is illumined the day,
And the wrecks of the ages in glory adorning ;
Till in peans of gladness all nature is voicing,
And the wail of the weeper is lost in rejoicing,
And the mother croons low to the babe on her breast,
"The angels will guard thee in peace to thy rest.
Sleep, little one, sleep ; you are brooded alway."

For placid and blue is the ocean eternal,
Where an island of souls lies forever and fair,
Where the palm trees of hope blossom deathless and vernal,
Where the sands of the ages in bright heaps are drifted,
And the domes of the city immortal are lifted,

And white ships lift anchor, and pass and repass,
Trail silent their sails o'er its bosom of glass,
And the mariner knows never tempest or care.

And ever and aye, when our hearts are aweary
With sorrows too heavy for mortals to bear,
And the desert of life becomes arid and dreary,
When our hearts have grown bitter with constantly breaking,
Lo! our angels return with love's sweet undertaking;
And soft as the falling of snow upon snows,
As the wing of the bee o'er the heart of the rose,
Is the tread of their feet on life's love-lighted stair

And we know that, whatever life's withering sorrow,
The good shall survive, that our dead live again!
O'er the darkest of nights wakes a happier morrow,
And the wrongs of the old in the new shall be righted,
And might with the right shall be justly united.
The world shall have learned it is better to give;
Through cycles eternal the spirit shall live;
And forever the angels are walking with men.

SAN FRANCISCO, CAL., March, 1885.

LOVE NEVER SLEEPS.

BELOVED, wheresoe'er thou art,
  In devious paths or distant lands,
The sacred angel of my heart
  With folded wing beside you stands.
When early o'er the eastern hills
  The gray sweet morning softly creeps,
And bird songs break in joyous thrills,
  Her shrine is yours. Love never sleeps.

When happy thou, her radiant smile
  Flings o'er me joy and hallowed peace;
If sad she finds your mood erewhile,
  My grief moans on without surcease.
If high meridian marks the noon,
  When cares distract, and turmoil sweeps
Down life's broad aisle, be this her boon,—
  To bless unseen. Love never sleeps.

When purpling lie the western skies,
   In orient gold and crimson-tipped
In sunset's glory-tinted dyes,
   While young night's scarf is passion-dipped,
As, homeward, clover-cropping kine
   Seek covert, and contentment keeps
In their corrals, so I to mine
   To pray for thee. Love never sleeps.

When brooding shadows dark o'ercast,
   In midnight fretted o'er with stars,
Waking, or dreaming o'er the past,
   Or future with its happier bars,
From early morn to set of sun,
   Till midnight's dew distills and weeps,
Till life through death submerged is won,
   Though dying, still Love never sleeps.

SAN FRANCISCO, CAL., July, 1884.

CONTENTMENT.

You may talk of the rolling prairie,
    With its billowy masses of green,
When a breeze o'er its surface is playing,
    It charms the beholder, I ween.

You may sigh for a tropical Eden,
    With its fragrant acacia and lime,
The shade of the orange and lemon,
    All the sweets of a sunnier clime.

You may list to the swell of the organ,
    As its thundering echoes prolong,
I have music that's sweeter and dearer
    Than the burthen of organ or song.

You may long for the wealth of the Indies,
    May sigh for a casket of gold,
But mine is a treasure more precious,
    Than all your vain riches tenfold.

My home is a cot on the hillside,
    That slopes to the lake-beaten shore,
And the races of snowy-winged vessels
    I can watch from my own cottage door.

Not mine are the palm and the plane tree,
    But mine are the maple and ash,
And they mingle their boughs on the hillside,
    O'er the margin where blue waters dash.

And mine is the music of voices,
    Sweet little boy voices—two,
With their four little roseate dimples,
    Four bright eyes of violet blue.

And mine—shall I mention my treasure?—
    Ah! yes, for it truly is mine,
And it fills me with infinite pleasure
    In devotion to bow at its shrine.

For I know that beneath the wide heavens,
    There warms at the call of my name,
A joy in the heart of another—
    Oh, Love is the treasure I claim.

CLIFTON, WIS., June, 1860.
Calumet Republican.

TO WINNEBAGO LAKE.

'Tis pleasant to glide o'er thy clear crystal bosom,
    As Phœbus ascends o'er yon towering cliff,
While pearls trickle down from our swift-plying paddles,
    And dancing waves kiss the smooth bow of our skiff.

How fragrant the breeze through the cottonwoods coming!
    How sweet thy soft cadence, ye murmuring rills!
How plaintive the echo, thou warbling minstrel,
    Of each dying note which thy feathered throat trills!

Oh, dear are thy waters, my loved Winnebago,
    And dear are thy banks where the night zephyrs play;
There first bloom the flowers that bid welcome the spring-time,
    And there the red oriole tunes his first lay.

And down to thy sand-sprinkled shore after school hours,
    Come little bare feet, tripping light on the spray,
And soft dimpled fingers, building castles of pebbles,
    Beguile the bright hours in their innocent play.

And sweet modest maidens, all radiant with blushes,
  Find shady retreat by thy whispering wave,
And twine in a circlet the wild forest blossoms,
  While, " wanton, thy waters their snowy feet lave."

Oh, had I the fire of a poet to number
  The praise which is due thee, in eloquent song,
And tune to the winds that sweep over thy surface,
  Bearing thy white crested wavelets along,

Or paint the rich splendor of crimson and azure,
  Which heightens thy charm as the day sinks to rest,
Or when Luna appears as the dim twilight deepens,
  To mirror her face on thy beautiful breast !

Let me sleep by thy soft swelling waves, Winnebago,
  When these limbs find repose in the slumber of death,
Where the whip-poor-will's song breaks the silence of evening,
  And the summer winds woo the wild violet's breath.

 CLIFTON, WIS., Sept. 1860.
  Calumet Republican.

TWO SIDES.

A knight in armor from the east,
Proudly bestrode his noble beast,
Attendant at a royal feast.

High o'er the arch that spanned the way,
Which caught the sun's reflecting ray,
A glittering shield was hung that day.

Another rider from the west,
Also in knightly armor dressed,
Approached, and guest saluted guest.

Up spoke the first with gesture bold:
"Sir Knight, God speed you, and behold
How beautiful this shield of gold!"

"Ah, beautiful! but you mistake;
The shield is of another make:
'Tis silver, I my life would stake."

"Indeed, Sir Knight, you do but jest,
'Tis plain my eyes do serve *me* best;
'Tis *gold*, and there we'll let it rest."

"Not so," the other hot replied.
"You do my vision so deride,
Your words imply that I have lied."

And so each sentence drew more fire,
Nor would they either one retire
Till they had spent their deadly ire.

And so it came about by chance,
Each on his neighbor drew his lance,
Nor recked the direful circumstance.

About that shield they slashed and swore,
Till, fainting, they could do no more
Than welter in each other's gore.

A runner from the castle's gate
Cried, "Out upon such sorry state!
Indeed, you'll make the dinner late.

"Excuse my breach of courtly rules,
But when, good sirs, your anger cools,
You'll both admit you were two fools.

"You could have spared this dire disgrace,
Had you but changed each one his place,
And met your host in better grace.

"Again, if I may be so bold,
That both were right each could have told;
That side is silver, this is gold."

MORAL.

'Tis ill-advised hot words to waste,
The proof of right to clog with haste,
For truth at times may be displaced.

SAN FRANCISCO, Nov. 30, 1892.

MY HEART WOULD HAVE ME LOVE YOU.

My heart would have me love you, dear,
  So warm its tender beating still must be.
Humid my lids with the unbidden tear
  Compassion weeps, to veil your thoughts from me.

You stand confessed before my soul's swift eyes,
  Yet make me weak excuses for your sin,
A plunderer of womanhood's dear prize,
  And hedge your weaknesses her own within.

So long your feet have wandered from the right
  You have forgot the ecstasy of love,
That hallowed flame whose soul-illumined light
  Alone doth burn on matehood's shrine above.

Than other men you are no worse, perhaps;
  You should be better, with your sense of wrong;
You know the downward pits from virtue's lapse
  That wait on woman, and you should be strong.

You call that love which angels count as lust,
  Yet woo your angel household to your side;
Love's sweet companionship you trail in dust,
  While love's dear recompense is crucified.

I count him not as guiltless who defiles
  The virgin birthright and love's wedded kiss,
Who, dallying, speeds the wanton lover's wiles,
  Who scorns to wed, yet robs another's bliss.

And so your soul, familiar grown with lust,
  Reads women all as those whom you consort.
Makes you insult true wifehood with distrust,
  And all its sacred ministry distort.

Think not my words are spoken to upbraid;
  My lips would rather kiss away your stain;
But think, dear heart, each weakling that has strayed
  Lays on some mother's heart the sword of pain.

To save your feet from treading out the wine
  The nightshade yields to poison life by stealth,
Love should bestow affection deep as mine,
  To win your angel from your grosser self.

For her sweet sake whose anguish gave you life,
   I would a later pain for you endure;
If through the agony of love's keen strife
   My heart might break, that yours be made more pure.

Did I not know you better than you seem,
   I might in sorrow turn my face away,
But just above your passion's turbid stream,
   The rainbow spans where purer waters play.

I stretch my hands above you and implore
   Heaven's holy ministers to guide your feet;
Lift up your eyes to where they walk before,
   And throbbing stars in your new dawn shall meet.

MELBOURNE, VICTORIA, Aug. 29, 1885.

THE END.

www.ingramcontent.com/pod-product-compliance
Lightning Source LLC
Chambersburg PA
CBHW021809230426
43669CB00008B/692